The Art *of* Home

The Art *of* Home

Shea McGee

HARPER HORIZON

To Syd, Wren, Ivy, and Margot—

Thank you for teaching me the true meaning of home.

The Art of Home

Copyright © 2023 Shea McGee and Syd McGee

All rights reserved. No portion of this book may be reproduced, stored in a retrieval system, or transmitted in any form or by any means—electronic, mechanical, photocopy, recording, scanning, or other—except for brief quotations in critical reviews or articles, without the prior written permission of the publisher.

Published by Harper Horizon, an imprint of HarperCollins Focus LLC.

Any internet addresses, phone numbers, or company or product information printed in this book are offered as a resource and are not intended in any way to be or to imply an endorsement by Harper Horizon, nor does Harper Horizon vouch for the existence, content, or services of these sites, phone numbers, companies, or products beyond the life of this book.

ISBN 978-0-7852-3685-6 (ebook)
ISBN 978-0-7852-3683-2 (HC)

Library of Congress Control Number: 2023933276

Printed in China

23 24 25 26 27 IMA 10 9 8 7 6 5 4 3 2 1

Contents

Introduction

Introduction

What I love about design is the opportunity to dream and then to will that vision into existence.

Thursday nights were free at the Museum of Fine Arts, and my dad would often load my brother and me into the back of our boxy red Volvo and head east toward downtown Houston. We'd wander around staring at works from Van Gogh, Monet, Manet, Pollock, or whatever the current exhibit had in store for us. As kids, we didn't know who the artists were or what techniques were employed, but we knew which pieces made us linger a little longer. The backdrops, color palettes, materials, and presentation impacted the way we felt when we were in their presence. Some artists made it look easy and others wanted you to see their painstaking attention to detail. Each piece was unique, a reflection of the artist and era. Years later, I realize that those Thursday nights spent walking through the museum with my dad were more than a history lesson; they were my first lessons in design.

Just as a few tools and an understanding of basic techniques give an artist a foundation from which to create, a home is a canvas and it is my role as a designer to pick up the brush and bring it to life. What I love about design is the opportunity to dream and then to will that vision into existence. In a way, that is exactly how I became an interior designer.

I've always had an interest in personal style and creating beauty in my surroundings, but it wasn't until after I graduated from college with a degree in communications that I discovered my true passion was interior design. Syd and I were newlyweds living in Southern California, and making our one-bedroom apartment feel like home consumed my attention. By day I worked at a marketing agency, but at night I devoured every magazine, catalog, blog, and design book I could find. Most weekends were spent thrifting and convincing Syd to tackle projects like painting cabinets and hanging artwork. He was reluctant; I was obsessed.

As we checked items off our to-do list and filled our hand-me-down IKEA sofa with new pillows, seeing the finished product only fueled my desire to continue creating. Deep down, I regretted that moment freshman year when I dropped my Intro to Interior Design course last minute because I was afraid to fail the drawing portion. (Drawing was, and still is, not my strong suit.) A few years later, with Syd's encouragement, I found myself staring down yet another Intro to Interior Design class, but this time it was at our local community college, and I completed the course.

While I was in design school, we bought our first home, and it became my proving ground as an interior designer, if only for myself. I started knocking out our kitchen cabinets within the first week. What started as a kitchen reno snowballed into all the main rooms in the home. I began documenting the progress on social media, which was a new concept for interior designers at the time, and I landed my first client. One client grew to a full roster, and I dropped out of design school and dove headfirst into building my business.

Within a year, I changed careers, started a new business, and had our first baby. After much deliberation, Syd and I decided to go into business together. We took a leap of faith, sold our beloved home and most of our belongings in San Clemente, California, and moved to Salt Lake City, Utah, to launch Studio McGee.

What started out of a spare bedroom has grown into a team of a few hundred people and a portfolio of projects spanning the country. My first design job was styling a set of bookshelves. The bookshelves turned into rooms, which turned into decorating full homes and eventually working alongside architects and builders to design high-end custom homes and remodels from the ground up. Now, Studio McGee encompasses not only home design but also content creation; a Netflix show, *Dream Home Makeover*; product development with our retail business, McGee & Co.; and multiple partnerships with brands like Target and Kohler.

As a designer, I have the opportunity to paint the backdrop of my clients' lives. I get to understand the nuances of their personal style, interests, and day-to-day routines so we can translate those into something tangible. Design has the ability to shape the way we feel in our homes. With each project and obstacle, I have come to see my role as part problem solver and part artist. With every room and every decision, I am continually devoted to developing my craft as an interior designer.

Nearly a decade has passed since I printed my first business card, and I have been balancing on that point where form meets function ever since. Digging in to the purpose and dreaming of the possibilities is one of my favorite parts of the process.

I am now and always have been a homebody. I am happiest when I am home. Creating a comfortable environment for my family is what hooked me in the beginning and why

I am still just as passionate about it hundreds of homes later. I am in my element when elevating our surroundings for myself and others. Whether it's tidying up, hosting dinner, or daydreaming about what project I'm tackling next, focusing on the way a home feels is what most energizes me.

My penchant for curating an aesthetic is an integral part of our family dynamic and lifestyle. Syd and I choose dinner in the backyard over dinner out most nights, and at the end of our fast-paced days, there is nowhere we'd rather be than home. Our kids love to invite friends over to the house, and our door is always open. We have also opened our home to the world in many ways, including via production crews, photo shoots, and social media content. However, when the cameras leave, it's not a set to us; it's back to dishes in the sink, bedtime routines, and working to uplift those within its walls and those outside of them.

When Syd encouraged me to start posting to Instagram all those years ago, I invited my small but growing audience into our home—sharing the progress, decisions, and lessons learned along the way. Early in my career, my mind was constantly pulled between considering aesthetics and recalling the technicalities of design implementation through the construction and installation process, learning through trial and error along the way. I have discovered that the more intuitive the rules of design have become, the freer my mind is to create (and the more confident I feel when breaking those rules).

The wonderful thing about design is that the principles can be applied to any size, scale, or style. With each home, our goal is to always understand how our clients live, pinpoint their style, and then design through the Studio McGee lens, which is beautifully balanced interiors with a perpetual sense of calm. From practical tips to notes on what makes the designs work, this book is a collection of our projects and a visual guide of lessons I've learned. My hope is that I can take some of the guesswork out of the process for you, thus making space for the freedom to create more beauty in your own home. Every room, hallway, or blank wall is an opportunity for what I like to call a "moment." A scene within a scene, it is a vignette comprising a curated compilation of pieces and architectural details that evoke a feeling.

Every home we design at Studio McGee follows a similar path: we begin with a jumble of ideas and move forward to reality, with a thousand decisions and obstacles along the way.

Home design should be enjoyable, but the sheer number of decisions can be overwhelming. I begin this book by sharing the road map I follow to create homes that embody the dreams of those that live within them. From there, I will take you on a room-by-room tour with best practices for tackling future design projects. Each chapter begins with my own home and follows with a curated selection of images from a few of my favorite projects through the years. In each, I share challenges we worked through, highlight the noteworthy details, and include tips that can help you in your own design projects.

When I was starting my journey as one of the first design influencers, I made a conscious decision to break the mold and lift the curtain on the design world. Over the years, I have stayed true to that vision of teaching and inspiring others to design their own homes. At the end of this book, you will find my style guide, a visual resource for design and decorating. It includes everything from how high to hang a light fixture and my go-to paint colors, to styling bookshelves and selecting the right rug for your space. I hope you immerse yourself in the imagery, learn something new, and enjoy the journey that is *The Art of Home*.

Design has the ability to shape the way we feel in our homes.

The Process

CHAPTER 01

The Process

Design is a process. It unfolds one step, one decision, and one layer at a time.

Design is a process. It unfolds one step, one decision, and one layer at a time. Although the end result of every design is unique to the home itself, the flow of how we at Studio McGee get there follows a similar framework. For me, every project, both large and small, begins with a mood board that sets a stylistic direction to work toward. This is the overarching goal. And the end of a project is what you make of it—styling the shelves, inviting family to the table, or open-ended shifting and tweaking as you, or your clients, live in the space. Everything in between is fluid, developing and adapting depending on the scope and needs of the project, the obstacles you run up against, and the mind-changing and mistakes that will inevitably come.

I prefer to begin working with our full-scale projects long before the air compressors *ping* and the trucks arrive to pour the foundation. Starting to collaborate—with architects, builders, zoning committees, and so on—this early in the process allows us to have a cohesive vision on how we want the home to feel in the end. When I unroll a 24-inch-by-36-inch architectural plan across my worktable, my mind immediately jumps to how each space will be filled in the end—a built-in nook versus a bench, a sectional versus a sofa,

a round coffee table versus a square one, an indoor/outdoor rug in a high-traffic space. Architects will look at the same set of lines and see an entirely different path forward; I am in awe of that skill set. If designers miss the opportunity for collaboration, we are handed a set of plans and asked to add lipstick.

The real magic happens when each team member is given the space for their expertise to shine, while being open to some give-and-take. At Studio McGee, we have been fortunate to collaborate with many talented architects, builders, and craftspeople, working to turn drawings and spreadsheets and dreams into reality. When the mood, architecture, and interior designs are thoughtfully and cohesively considered, they'll elevate one another. If I've learned anything, it's that great design is born out of collaboration.

With that said, not every home design requires an entire team or demolition. Beyond that, not every homeowner is prepared with the time and resources to tackle their entire home simultaneously. Regardless, our design process will carry you through our mindset when bringing an entire home, a single room, or a simple corner to life.

At the beginning of a project, it is easy to feel overwhelmed by the sheer number of decisions that go into making a home—it's hundreds, maybe even thousands—and the order in which to make them. One mistake can feel incredibly daunting. Over time and through many mistakes of my own, I have established a design process that allows the entire project to flow, making it much easier to feel invigorated by the possibilities. This process doesn't guarantee the lack of mistakes—those will still happen—but rather arms you with the best tools for lessening their gravity. Every project presents unique challenges, but this outline will help you pace yourself as you build both confidence and a beautiful home. Have courage in your vision, embrace the process, and relish the art of making a house feel like home.

STEP NO. 01

Mood

STEP NO. 02

Architecture

STEP NO. 03

Design Board

STEP NO. 04

Finishes

STEP NO. 05

Furniture

STEP NO. 06

Styling

STEP Nº. 1

Mood

Home is a feeling. Whether you're designing an entire estate or overhauling your kitchen, establishing how you want a home to feel is always the first step. We create mood boards before we make a single selection or drawing for a project.

A mood board is not a design board. This is where we comb through hundreds of saved images and narrow them to a select few, establish a color palette, add abstract inspiration, and incorporate direction for materials.

Mood boards are my North Star to establish the aesthetic direction of a project and communicate that vision with our clients and team members. The intent is to create alignment to inform decision-making throughout the rest of the process. Early in my career, I assumed that speaking with clients and reviewing their saved images was enough to kick off a project. But I discovered that clients would save widely differing images than the words used to describe their dream home. Visuals speak louder than words in design—every person's version of "traditional" or "modern" or "neutral" is unique.

---

01 Gather imagery

Use Pinterest or good old-fashioned magazine tears to gather every photo that speaks to you.

---

02 Look for themes

Ask yourself, *What are the themes that emerge through colors, textures, and details?* Those themes are the best indicators of your personal style—things you gravitate toward time and time again.

---

03 Edit

For each space you are designing, narrow down five to seven images that work in harmony when placed next to one another.

---

04 Create cohesion

Be sure your mood board includes the following:

- At least one wide room shot of an inspiration room
- Detail photos
- Color swatches
- Material textures
- Inspiration from unexpected places like landscapes or travel photography

Architecture

The "bones" of a home are the framework from which we design the interiors. I'm not an architect, but as a designer I'm intimately involved with the architecture of the home. My goal is to understand the architectural language and speak to the style, location, and homeowner's personal taste. Every decision should highlight and elevate the structure in a way that draws you in through form, flow, and attention to detail. This includes every choice— from the style of baseboards, to the cabinetry, to the wood species used on a vaulted ceiling.

However, the architectural process isn't always about adding to the structure. It's about thoughtfully considering what to leave out or take away. In remodels, we often remove walls and fussy flourishes that are not allowing the space to breathe. In contemporary homes, we will intentionally omit window casings or cabinet hardware for a more streamlined look.

If you live in a tract-style community or your home is simply lacking architectural interest, looking for ways to add architectural details is one of the first things you can do to improve both the style and value of your home. Although I'm a big believer in the power of a new throw pillow, no amount of pillow styling can fix poor architecture, which is why this step is critical to the process even if you are not building from the ground up.

TIP: Flow is thinking beyond the hallways. Consider things like window placement and future furniture layout.

01 Drawings

Whether you learn a program like AutoCAD or SketchUp, or you grab a piece of graph paper and a pencil, drawings to scale help clearly communicate how to bring your ideas to life. From reviewing the architectural plans to creating spatial layouts or elevations for cabinetry, drawings are a crucial step in getting your home right. Don't be afraid to get out a pen, mark up your plans, and sketch out the details.

02 Function

Carefully consider how each space, corner, and drawer will be used. The planning phase is the easiest time to make adjustments. As you move throughout the space in question, keep notes about what is easy and flag the pain points.

03 Flow

I like to close my eyes and mentally walk through the home to imagine how each space will work and connect.

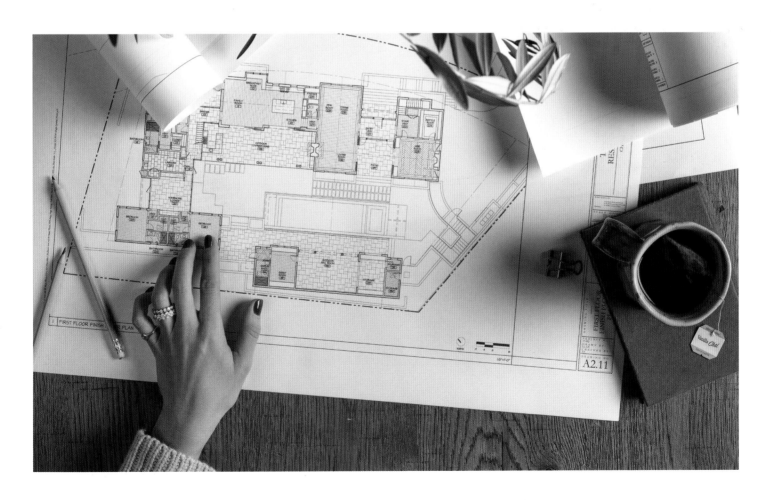

Design Board

The design board is where the actual selections for the project happen. I prefer to work digitally so I can pull a plethora of options and see how they work together in harmony. Unlike a mood board, which is abstract and directional, your design board should be more thorough and specific.

Although many designers select finishes and furniture at the same time, I create design boards for finishes first to get the ball rolling and stay on track for project timelines, and then I focus on furniture when the home is in the framing stage. This allows me to stand in the unfinished rooms and "feel" how they will come to life with furniture. Beyond imagery, I also like to incorporate notes on design boards to clarify details for our clients and contractors.

This is an exciting step toward seeing your vision become a reality, and it is an incredibly effective tool for communicating with the artisans working on a project.

Finishes

Finishes are the selections that bring dimension and interest to the structure of the home. After we create elevation drawings in black and white, we add the color through the materials and product choices.

The finishes should speak to the architecture while simultaneously laying the foundation for "soft" selections such as furniture and decor. These selections are big-ticket items with less flexibility to swap out later, so I prefer to focus on styles that have timeless staying power with subtle accents of trending elements.

We often refer to finishes as "hard" materials, which include the following:

Flooring

Trim work

Cabinetry

Countertops

Plumbing

Tile

Walls

Paint

Lighting

Hardware

Furniture

Picking rugs and furniture was how I originally fell in love with design, and it is still the most enjoyable part of the experience for me. My role at Studio McGee reaches beyond selections and now encompasses the design direction and creation for our own line of furniture for McGee & Co. The depth of a sofa or shape of a leg—it is fascinating to me how the subtleties of furniture influence the style of an entire room. I also find comfort in the organic and ever-evolving nature of furniture. If your furniture feels stale after a few years, making a few simple swaps can have an enormous impact without a complete overhaul. Unlike tile or countertops, furniture is flexible—have an open mind to rearranging or rotating items within or between rooms. Preparation and planning will help you avoid expensive mistakes and feel confident in your investments. Here are five tips when it comes to the furniture phase of the design process.

01 Start with a jumping-off point

Some designers begin with rugs and others with artwork. There is no right or wrong answer. The most important thing is that you start with what inspires you and build from there.

02 Measure twice and buy once

There are many online tools to draw your furniture layout to scale. (Graph paper works well too.) Place larger pieces first and then fill in with accents like lamps and side tables. I like to draw out the plan and then tape it on the floor using painter's tape. This allows you to "walk" around the furniture to see how it feels in the actual space.

03 Mix and match

Go beyond furniture sets and create furniture pairings with a balanced approach. Keep in mind that opposites attract—pair a sleek lamp with a traditional chair or a vintage accent table with a new sofa.

04 Scale is just as important as style

Weave together a story of both large and small selections. Scale is about the relationship between pieces and with the space as a whole. Juxtaposing sizes creates visual impact and allows the eye to move throughout the room.

05 Good things take time

Quality furniture takes time to make, and finding the perfect antique piece does not happen overnight. Create a plan but allow for pivots along the way. In the end, the changes often end up being my favorite part of the design. The best rooms unfold over time—even for professionals.

Styling

The decor tells your story—it's the photo from your wedding, the crock for wooden spoons you found at the thrift shop, and the plaid pillow you are loving right now. After you have created a solid architectural foundation and selected finishes and furniture to inspire living, styling is where you can really make a home your own. For a more collected look, gather meaningful accents throughout the process to be incorporated when the project is complete. Here are five things I take into consideration when styling:

01 **Composition**	A good stylist takes into consideration how objects—whether alone or stacked—relate to one another.
02 **Personality**	Sentimental items and vintage finds bring character and charm.
03 **Material**	Sleek surfaces and natural elements bring texture.
04 **Size**	Mix the scale of your decor through size and levels.
05 **Variety**	Create interest by varying the principles above.

Have courage in your vision,
embrace the process,

*and relish the art of making
a house feel like home.*

Entryways

CHAPTER 02

Entryways

I like to think of an entryway like a greeting . . . that first impression sets the tone for the entire experience.

The moment you cross the threshold into a home's entryway, you are handed the visual keys to how the rest of the space will unfold. Whether you're greeted by soaring ceilings and a winding staircase or a scatter rug and a few hooks on the wall, every home has an opportunity to make an entrance. I like to think of an entryway like a greeting: you can be welcomed with a warm hug or a handshake—but that first impression sets the tone for the entire experience.

In our first apartment, the floor plan did not have a dedicated entry. In fact, you could see the dining room, kitchen, living room, laundry, and bedroom all from our front porch. There was, however, a small wall that extended a few feet beyond the front door. I laid down a 2-foot-by-3-foot rug, mounted a coatrack, and hung a piece of thrifted artwork, and with those few small additions our tiny allotment of extra wall space became an entrance.

In our current home, I had my heart set on a vaulted ceiling in the great room. The lofty aesthetic of such a large space influenced decisions I made elsewhere in my home. I wanted to bring some intimacy into the entry experience. To do so, I carried the painted brick from our home's exterior onto the interior walls of the entry and intentionally opted for lower

ceilings and a small footprint. Walking through our front door and under the barrel arch, you're greeted with warmth while also given a hint of the grand space that soars beyond the opening. An antique console table juxtaposed with an oversized lamp provides the push and pull between inviting and luxe that I hoped to achieve throughout our home.

When designing an entryway, think beyond what you want the space to say and consider instead what it says about the rest of your home. This perspective will inform your decisions and how to greet your guests through the design.

As my portfolio of work with Studio McGee has grown over the years, so have the footprints of the homes and their respective entries. Our aim is to create an all-encompassing sensory experience when you walk through the front door. We consider the clients' lifestyles and whether the intent is to impress or to feel cozy.

Although styles and statements vary, furniture needs and combinations are often similar—think console vignette, mirror, bench seating, or a round foyer table. Perhaps formulaic in plan, what happens next is creating an introduction to your home through pieces that speak to your style and the way you live.

Choose a focal point, typically the largest piece in the room, and build from there. I love mirrors in an entry for many reasons—they draw your eye in, bounce light around, and give people a chance to do a quick glance on their way in and out of the door.

You can incorporate molding details or a texture like wood, stone, or brick, but I find it most impactful to incorporate materials in entryways that bridge the exterior and interior of the home in either a literal or abstract way.

TIP: Carry the exterior-door color inside for a simple way to connect the outside to the inside while simultaneously creating a grand appearance.

When designing this home in Marin County, California, we used repetition of the oak beams and iron lanterns to highlight the length rather than attempt to disguise its hallway-like features. A twelve-foot console is centered by an expansive gold mirror to bring a formal flair to collected finds like the antique jar lamps, an unframed oil painting, and French laundry baskets.

TIP: We often use vintage rugs in entryways to center the space and add color, pattern, and eclecticism—all while hiding dirt.

The grounding nature of organic materials resonates deep within us on a visual and emotional level. Stained-wood paneling creates a sense of intimacy with the large-scale steel windows. When styling a console, pay attention to varying heights. When furniture space is limited but the room is calling for an additional layer, think no further than the floor—ottomans, a low plant, or sculptural objects add a lot without stealing square footage.

The grounding nature of organic materials resonates deep within us on a visual and emotional level.

TIP: Molding details, flooring, lighting, and even a floral arrangement—each decision in an entryway sets the tone for your home, down to the scent of the candles.

For this modern mountain home in Victory Ranch, Utah, an open-concept entry with double-sided fireplace called for a round table to fill the space. We drew inspiration from the scenic painting above the mantel and paired it with bleached oak, a rustic jar, and olive-green suede ottoman layered below.

TIP: Hide rugs are a great solution for irregular floor plan shapes.

When we began working on this project, the entryway was an afterthought built as a connection point between the original 1800s pioneer home and the 1970s addition. When square footage isn't doing the talking, let other details speak for you. We focused on bringing drama to the walls with a patterned wallpaper that served as our inspiration for the entire remodel. We color-matched the green leaves in the wallpaper to the contrast trim with an integrated peg rail for hanging hats, coats, and bags. The one piece of furniture we were able to nestle into the space was an antique that had faded to the exact background color of the wallpaper.

TIP: A chest provides additional storage and also acts as a drop zone for keys and sunglasses.

50   HISTORIC CHARLESTON REMODEL, UTAH

Living Rooms

CHAPTER 03

Living Rooms

The living room is often at the intersection of our daily lives and pivotal moments.

They say the heart of the home is the kitchen, but I think the real living begins in the living room. This is where we gather, we settle in, we lounge, and we play. For some, their floor plans offer differentiated formal and informal living rooms, but for many, a single living room is the backdrop for moments both large and small. It seems like one moment we're building a blanket fort and the next we're arranging fresh flowers and placing a tray of hors d'oeuvres on the coffee table for guests. In our home, the living room serves as the headquarters of our family and is where our home truly feels like home.

Decorating the living room in our first apartment as newlyweds was when I first started to feel a pull into the world of design. I would sit on our hand-me-down IKEA sectional tearing out pages of magazines, earmarking design books, and dreaming that I would one day have the courage to call myself a designer. More than a decade later, I'm once again sitting in our home's living room, but this time on a sofa that I designed, in a home I conceptualized from the ground up, and it's me that is writing the design book. The living room is often at the intersection of our daily lives and the pivotal moments that shape it.

My vision for our dream living room started with a vintage hand-knotted rug I found in North Carolina about four years before we even knew where or when we'd be building a home. It featured a perfectly faded blue-and-tan pattern that I just couldn't get out of my mind. The rug was about two times too large for our rental home at the time, but I bought it without telling Syd and then kept it rolled up in a corner of our crawl space, schlepping it between rentals until the time was just right.

When the time came, I designed our living room to have soaring ceilings with exposed wood trusses and a wall of doors that opened to the backyard. With the magnitude of the ceiling, I wanted to balance the grandeur with a fireplace that exuded warmth and coziness. This room is an embodiment of the tension between selections that bring depth to a design—linen and velvet, jute and oak, steel and brass.

The give-and-take between comfort and style is where good living rooms shine. In our projects at Studio McGee, I strive to create an air of elevated livability. The real secret is in the mix. High and low, old and new, curvy and straight—you could be in a penthouse apartment or a beach bungalow and this approach would land you in the sweet spot of lofty yet down-to-earth design.

Our living room is a study in juxtaposition as a reflection of the way we use the space. Our main sofa is luxuriously deep and perfect for lounging—it's upholstered in Crypton performance fabric for maximum durability. The fawn-colored velvet sofa is a piece I had been daydreaming about manufacturing, and the prototype lives in our home. The curved back is more formal than its counterpart and looks beautiful from all angles. The seating is a delicate balance to the custom steel built-ins flanking the fireplace.

TIP: Don't forget to pay attention to the back side of chairs when they're placed in clear view. These angled cane-back chairs look great from all sides.

Warm wood cathedral ceilings and awe-inspiring steel windows set the tone in this sitting room. Our client was set on straying from the beach themes prevalent in the area, so we drew inspiration from their time spent in Napa.

The sweeping arms of the iron chandelier served as a starting point to incorporate subtle curves throughout the space. These soft curves are manifested in the corner detail of the wallpaper-backed built-ins, traditional Persian rug, reeded details on the coffee table, and even the tufted sofa. Despite the grandeur, the room is still welcoming thanks to casually layered artwork over the mantel, ticking-stripe spindle chairs, and eclectic styling. Interpreting the inspiration in understated ways ties the room together but also allows for flexibility in the design.

Interpreting the inspiration in understated ways ties the room together but also allows for flexibility in the design.

TIP: By incorporating remarkable finishes—like a stone fireplace surround or stained beams—you can create an awe-inspiring backdrop to layer in furniture that invites people to relax and stay awhile.

In our Crestview Project, a full-scale remodel in San Diego, the goal was to create a clean-lined yet organic living space to bridge the indoors and out.

We worked with the architect to carry a theme of warm white oak through the ceiling, floors, windows, and trim of the built-in shelves. We designed the plaster fireplace to recess inward rather than the traditional step forward, and the hearth is a slab of rough-faced stone that stands proudly alone. So proud, in fact, that at the end of the process we recognized this moment was art in and of itself and opted to forgo a mantel for artwork.

This room has two focal points—the fireplace and the view—so we oriented the furniture to feel comfortable facing both directions. Ink-blue and stone-washed grays in the furnishings offer a cool balance to the warm finishes.

Simplicity is a feeling created by hundreds of nuanced details.

Situated high in the Rocky Mountains, this vacation home was designed with its surroundings in mind. With snowcapped mountains, rusty-red rocks, and a nearby lake, the terrain is felt in every texture, color, and design decision in this living room. We worked with the architect to mix rough-sawn timbers with soft furnishings for a push and pull between rustic and light.

Our client wanted a clean and neutral aesthetic, so we looked for places to create consistency and repetition. Here, we carried the stain of the floors to the cabinetry in the kitchen as well as the living- and dining-room furniture. We even applied the concept in matching the hardware finish to the chandelier.

Even if you're designing a single space at a time, consider sight lines from one room to the next rather than only thinking about the room you're designing. This will create a more connected and intentional feeling in your home.

TIP: A solid-marble accent table in a sculptural shape serves as art and a place to rest your glass.

This living room in Rye, New York, was designed for a trusting client with one very specific request: keep it modern and keep it black and white. In this remodel, we raised the floor of what was once a sunken living space to create a connected lounge, living room, and dining room. The built-in bar area helps bring purpose, a focal point, and fun to a large wall.

This new-traditional home for a young family in Arizona was designed to stand the test of time with selections that speak to both old and current eras. This was the more formal of the two living spaces in the home and needed to bridge life with toddlers and sitting pretty.

We accomplished this through elevated finishes, such as the subtle arches with brass cremone bolts on the glass-front built-ins and a wide-reaching brass chandelier. The ceiling trusses could have taken the design to a more rustic place, but we opted to paint them a soft putty color, allowing some of the knots and imperfections to show through for character. A few intentionally casual moments, like the cane daybed and seagrass coffee table, bring approachability to this living room. It's no secret that I love a calming palette, but the secret is not about a lack of color—it's about toning it down so that you avoid the "pops."

My favorite addition to the room, however, is not something we designed or purchased; it is the pair of spindle chairs from our clients' alma mater, where they met attending medical school. Hours of shopping and drawing could never match what a well-placed sentimental piece brings to a home.

When designing in a new-traditional style, we start with a foundation of symmetry and then shake it up. Here, the fireplace design, room shape, and pairs of chairs give us a traditional base, and the rest of the furniture and decor is mixed and matched to bring a fresh perspective to traditional design.

TIP: Consistent metal finishes create flow from one room to the next even as the paint colors change.

It's no secret that I love a calming palette, but the secret is not about a lack of color—

it's about toning it down so that you avoid the "pops."

When designing a new home, it is typical to begin with decisions about the exterior materials or the kitchen, which then influence all subsequent choices. In this home, however, the wine room came first. Decidedly both old school and new school, the room reflects our intent to set a mood and design a space with heart.

TIP: A glass table lends space to a cozy arrangement and allows the pattern of the rug to shine through.

A few months after wrapping up a vacation home for our client, we received a call that they had purchased a property high in the hills of Marin County with views of the Pacific. Building a home is not for the faint of heart, but they were ready to embark on another journey with us even though the punch list on their vacation home was barely complete.

We'd already built trust with the client, who had a penchant for warm neutrals and a moody aesthetic, so we took the direction and ran with it. I always look for opportunities to incorporate a few loud moments between the quiet. The heavily veined marble plinth table, the funky little lamp with pleated shade, and the blue-black painted fireplace maintain the intended aesthetic while pushing the design to another level.

A little "grandma" goes a long way. Vintage details like floral, pleats, or even fringe help a design stay away from feeling specific to one time period and give personality to any space—even modern ones.

Tonal layers complement without competing with the stone walls in this Napa Valley estate. Nubby chairs and relaxed slipcovered sofas are grounded by a stately raked-edge coffee table and jute rug. We styled this great room with two symmetrical slipcovered sofas to divide the long, open space into zones to avoid a bowling alley effect.

An old pioneer home is both honored and revived with vintage finds and new furniture and finishes. Our client was at a loss for how to speak to the history of the home while also providing updated living accommodations for their family of six. We restored the original pine floors, reimagined the fireplace surround with over-grouted masonry, and added reclaimed beams and trim from a nearby farm. A blank wall served as a canvas of sorts for hanging cowbells reminiscent of the original owner's dairy farm.

TIP: When your ceiling is too low for a central fixture, try a grid of flush mounts to make a statement.

Adding warmth and comfort to contemporary homes is one of my favorite challenges, and it's all about softening the structured lines with a mix of textures and curves in all the right places. Our client requested a soft palette, so our goal was to add as much interest as possible through layers of materials.

TIP: When working with a muted color palette, zoom in to the details and bring dimension to every vignette with intentionally layered styling pieces.

Kitchens

CHAPTER 04

Kitchens

By mixing the function with the art of design, we can make the heart of the home feel special.

When I was growing up, Sundays after church were for baking. My mom would pull out a binder of recipes taken from *Southern Living* that were scribbled on note cards and stuck in sheet protectors caked with flour and little droplets of butter. I'd sit on the counter and sneak brown sugar and wait for my turn to use the mixer. I now share this same ritual with my daughters, plopping them up on the island, eating too much cookie dough, and rotating whose turn it is to measure and pour. By the time we pull our Sunday treat out of the oven, we're usually so full from snacking that we just pick at the dessert.

Recently, I found myself scolding the girls for not waiting until the recipe was complete, but I stopped short when I realized that the dessert wasn't the point—it was the time spent together in the kitchen. Whether we were cooking or not, many of my memories with loved ones are tied to moments with them in the kitchen. From the feel of your favorite wood spoon to the smell of fresh-baked bread, a kitchen envelops all our senses, leaving indelible impressions in our minds. As the beautiful scenery for those memories, the kitchen is one of the most important spaces in a home and a jumping-off point for designing all the other rooms thereafter.

When Syd and I were developing our floor plan, I wanted the island to be the heart of the kitchen. I envisioned myself serving most meals there, while also seeing into our living room and backyard while cooking. Perhaps living in many rentals without the luxury of an island led me to overcompensate when we designed our home, but we landed on a thirteen-and-a-half-foot island large enough to accommodate our entire family.

I went through many iterations of our island before deciding on the one. Much of what I share in this book is practical and tactical, but a huge part of design is instinctual—always listen to your gut. I had a specific vision for the range wall in our kitchen that included a Chantilly-white and brass Lacanche range from France, plaster hood, and a single floating shelf suspended between tall cabinets. It was perfect—symmetrical and balanced, closed and open, statement-making and functional. However, it was so perfect that when designing the island, repeating the symmetry just felt wrong—*too* perfect and not thoughtful enough. Too much perfection in design feels flat. I tried leg details, countertop profiles, and drawer layouts all to no avail. When things are just not coming together, it's time to step away from the screen and sleep on it.

I came back with fresh eyes and erased the idea that the island needed symmetry—what it needed was large open shelves on one end of the island, which pushed the stools off-center and gave me space to store my mismatched piles of collected bread bowls, cookbooks, and serveware. The concept of light cabinets with a dark island is not groundbreaking, but being intentional with details sets the design apart from the rest.

Beyond the cabinetry design, it's the materials that make a kitchen. It's easy to want everything crafted from indestructible man-made materials, but selecting a few natural materials (or at least one if you're hesitant) with patina gives a kitchen authenticity and staying power—think stone counters, living finishes on the plumbing and hardware, wood textures, and backsplashes with natural character. Our kitchen incorporates all of those elements, and the etching of our Calacatta marble countertops and the aging of our brass faucets is beautiful and speaks to the enduring quality of those materials, which have been used in design for hundreds of years.

The kitchen is a multipurpose hub used from sunup to sundown for cooking, eating, and hanging out. By no means is a beautiful kitchen an indication of culinary talent or the quality of time spent together. We don't need to be a professional chef or prepare a complicated recipe to enjoy special moments in the kitchen. Regardless of our varying skill levels, we always aim to create a welcoming space to gather and cook up memories. By mixing the function with the art of design, we can make the heart of the home feel special.

TIP: Mixing countertop thicknesses and edge profiles is a great way to achieve a more designer look.

Adding sconces and petite accent lighting for ambience brings a thoughtful layer to the kitchen, and it works in any style, new or old, modern or traditional.

This classic kitchen hits all the right notes for never going out of style. White cabinets? Check. Soapstone counters? Check. Polished-nickel faucet and hardware? Check, check. Timeless materials never grow old as long as we drive the minutiae forward. The integrated hood, brick niches, weathered zinc lanterns, and decorative hardware on the apron sink bring originality to the design and keep your eye moving throughout the space.

TIP: You will never regret taking the tile all the way to the ceiling. When the light reflects off the tile, it brings your kitchen to life.

This contemporary new-build kitchen was an exercise in bringing interest to simple forms. Our client loved clean lines and light wood tones, a theme carried throughout this entire home for continuity. With the room's double islands and an open-concept floor plan where one could see the hearth room, nook, dining room, great room, and entry all from the kitchen sink, the challenge was to keep the simplicity from becoming monotonous. We needed to create boldness without the use of a bold color. Playing with proportion, mixing metals, and blending warm and cool led us to create the centerpiece of this kitchen.

When you have all the right ingredients, it's hard to go wrong in the kitchen. Calacatta marble, Waterworks fixtures, a French range, and cascading plaster hood work together for a harmonious result. Given the warmth of the ceiling and floors, we opted for monochromatic painted cabinetry with a raised-panel profile. The unexpected traditionalism of the cabinets sits comfortably with the sleek slab backsplash and steel windows.

Through the glass panes of the antique pocket door, you capture a glimpse of the deep-charcoal cabinetry and soapstone counters in the pantry. The contrast feels like the best kind of surprise in design—unexpected yet completely seamless with the overall design of the home.

Sometimes—in design and life—the best results come from pivots. In our original plans, the hood had enclosed sides that extended down to the countertops, and the island was centered on the range. However, when our client painted a picture of their family cooking at home in their individual kitchen zones, we shifted at the last minute to consider our client's love for family cooking and added more prep space. We eliminated the sides of the hood and added the butcher-block end detail to the side of the island, resulting in some of my favorite elements in the kitchen.

TIP: Approach imperfections in remodels as opportunities to create something special, like this butcher-block addition to the island that extends the surface and helps the off-center sink feel more intentional.

Sometimes—in design and life—

the best results come from pivots.

A custom home built on a twenty-acre working alfalfa farm, this expansive kitchen was designed with family and function in mind. Function is not just about practicality; it is about purpose. For some, their kitchens are designed as a showpiece and that is their function. For others, their kitchens are designed for ardent cooking and durability.

In this kitchen, the purpose was space—space for a family of seven and their future generations to gather, space for cooking, and space for hosting. Two islands fit the bill, and the inspiration followed. A time-honored palette of black and white is accented with a rich Jacobean stain and spindle-back stools.

Functionality is not just about practicality; it is about purpose.

Blue doesn't have to be exclusive to coastal design; it changes its mood depending on the setting. Painted cabinets are not the obvious choice in a mountain home where stained wood tones are more prevalent. However, we went against the grain and opted for steel-blue cabinets to bring depth of color and allow the stained beams, floor, and island countertop to stand apart.

After a tragic loss, this home was completed as a tranquil respite for our client's family. A cool palette is reminiscent of the snowcapped mountains through the windows, where the contrast of dark and light play together in the distance. The calming effect this kitchen has on the eyes is about the tension between addition and restraint.

TIP: Look for places to make your cabinetry feel more like furniture. A built-in hutch offers a display for a mix of pieces, from glassware to special-occasion serveware and pretty cookbooks.

Arabescato marble steals the show in our basement kitchenette, extending from the countertop to the backsplash and onto a shelf suspended by unlacquered brass brackets from England. Oak cabinetry with kerf detailing connects old-world and modern design.

TIP: A single shelf can be as impactful as multiple shelves to display layers of collected items and decor.

We utilized the existing footprint of the original kitchen but remodeled every surface for a dramatic result that blends a high-contrast palette with engaging details.

This pool-house kitchen brings the outdoors in with a garage-style glass window and blue tile that speaks to the pool beyond.

TIP: If you can sacrifice the extra storage, a furniture-inspired island provides a visual reprieve.

Dining Rooms

CHAPTER 05

Dining Rooms

The nourishment extends beyond mealtime as it is a designated place to gather and spend time together.

When Syd and I sold our first home and moved into a rental to pursue building Studio McGee together, the dining table was the epicenter of both our family life and our business life. There was a small space between the kitchen and living room to squeeze in a round table and four chairs. We would clear our plates, put Wren—our oldest and only child at the time—down for her nap, and then crack open our laptops. We had one employee, and we would all speak in hushed tones hoping that the baby's nap would last long enough for us to be productive. Later, the screens would be cleared away, dinner would be served, and coloring books would take over the table.

Although we now have dedicated office space and working hours, the dining table is still at the center of connection for our family. Regardless of where we are in any given moment, the dining table is a reflection of our lives. The cleaner the table, the busier we tend to be, and it's a reminder to slow down and connect as a family. On its surface, a dining room is a place for nourishment. The nourishment, however, extends beyond mealtime as it is a designated place to gather and spend time together.

In our new home, we opted to blend the concepts of a formal dining area and kitchen nook to better suit our lifestyle. The shape of a dining room influences the shape of the table, and our dining room called for a long rectangle. However, with all the grids on the windows and ceiling,

I wanted to push beyond the obvious choice of straight lines. I designed a white oak racetrack-shaped table to give us length for hosting as well as a sense of softness that I felt the room was asking for. The mix of woven seating and upholstered end chairs blends casual and formal styles, so that with the quick addition of a tablecloth and place settings, our dining room transforms from Tuesday night dinner to Thanksgiving with the whole family.

Dining room layouts tend to be straightforward, so instead I focus my attention on creating visual contrast. Dressing the walls with color, trim, wallpaper, or windows sets the mood for the furniture selections, dictating what should go where and how it will play off other pieces. Just as you do when getting dressed in the morning, choose items that coordinate rather than match—it takes time but is worth the extra effort to ensure a thoughtfully curated style.

"A formal dining room that feels formal (but not too formal) and farmhouse (but not too farmhouse)" was the direction given when we set out to design this space made for entertaining. The vastness of the ceilings and wall space on either side of the ten-foot table called for variation in filling the empty space. On the side with the hutch, we focused on height, and on the opposite side we changed the level and paid attention to length. The key to balance in design is focusing on counterbalance. For every rustic piece in this dining room, like the antique buffet or weathered urn, there is a sleek choice, like the angular metal side chairs and chic glass taper candleholders. A room develops allure when juxtaposed elements sit comfortably together.

TIP: When a room has long walls, start with the weight in the center and build out to the sides.

The key to balance in design is

focusing on counterbalance.

Upon entering this home, you are greeted by an all-glass vestibule with views of the Rocky Mountains and little room for furniture. The dining room was designed as a nook off the main entry hall, making it the home's first opportunity to create an impression after a resident or guest takes in the surrounding landscape. We took great care to work with the architect and ensure this space had presence even if it only had two walls and was adjacent to a wide thoroughfare.

The beam layout became crucial in telling this story. Rippling drapes with a tonal pattern provided fullness to windowed walls, and furniture selections with a smooth grain offered visual reprieve from the rough texture of the timbers. Two large pendants in a simple cone shape added to the volume in a less-is-more way, which describes the statement we hoped to achieve in this dining room.

TIP: If you want to shake up your dining seating, don't be afraid to think beyond the end chairs. Here we designed two slipcovered benches to add low-profile softness to the space.

At the outset of this project, our clients came to us with a familiar request for their home: "We want it to feel light and airy." We designed the main living spaces, kitchen, and, originally, the dining room with this in mind. But I couldn't get it out of my head that the room design just wasn't there yet. About twenty-four hours before the room was to be painted, I frantically emailed our design team that we needed a jewel-box moment in this home. I find that light without the dark ceases to feel extraordinary and can quickly become monotonous. I look to smaller spaces for opportunities to surprise, and they often become our clients' favorite spaces in their homes. We pitched the idea of changing to charcoal-blue walls, and I'm grateful for our clients' trust in our vision.

TIP: Building a custom plate rack into the paneled walls keeps the feature fresh rather than dated.

The bold tones of the still life artwork in this dining room are both the focal point and the point of inspiration for the furniture and decor. A walnut-stained table is surrounded by barrel-back woven chairs and a comfortable settee for long evenings at the dinner table. A collection of stacked serving pieces is a homey choice for styling.

We decided to forgo a chandelier and focus on the styling in this dining area situated between the kitchen and living room. A vintage floral painting and pleated gingham pillows offer a playful touch to this cozy kitchen nook.

TIP: For comfortable placement, plan for the table to sit directly in line with, or one to two inches away from, the built-in seating.

A combined formal living and dining room is a familiar layout that requires careful consideration to create flow and individuality in each space. The immensity of the ceilings but only one narrow wall to decorate led us to focus primarily on the furniture. We stumbled upon these woven-leather and chrome dining chairs that tie in the oak ceilings and rich brown hues from other areas of the home. The strong hits of black in the artwork and accessories add drama and modernity to the tried-and-true bleached jute rug and relaxed barrel-back captain's chairs.

TIP: A trestle table is the smartest investment in a dining room. It pairs well with anything and can be dressed up or down depending on its surroundings.

Dining banquettes are charming by nature, even before adding the details. After placing the woven chairs and neutral pillows, I could not help but hang an off-kilter vintage art piece to add personality to the space. Details like these give contemporary homes more character while still maintaining their hallmark clean lines.

TIP: Add textural accents through furniture pieces, textiles, and even artwork to bring depth and warmth to white walls and minimal color palettes.

Bedrooms

CHAPTER 06

Bedrooms

Blending styles requires give-and-take but also connection.

A deep exhale, relaxed shoulders, and a mind at ease—this is the reaction I strive for in every bedroom we design at Studio McGee. How we reach that goal in each bedroom is as unique as the house itself. Accomplishing cohesion through contrasting elements requires careful consideration, but giving it an abundance of forethought will produce a room that feels like it was created with intent.

Not all designers seek peace and calm through their designs, but it is what I crave. My clients come to me with the same vision in their own homes. Serenity can be found through soothing color palettes as well as the tactile qualities of each surface. From the ceiling—the first thing we see when we open our eyes—to the texture of the sheets and the rug underfoot, it is the unspoken interactions with the materials around us that make it easy to relax our minds and bodies in the evenings and give us the energy to roll out of bed each morning.

My earliest bedroom designs were neither relaxing nor energizing. The first bedroom I styled was my dorm room: a twin mattress on cinder blocks with a desk as a nightstand. I folded a quilt at the end of my duvet, hung floating shelves, and placed black-and-white photos above the bed to distract from, well, everything. I carried those grainy photos I took

myself on a Kodak EasyShare digital camera from apartment to apartment until Syd and I got married and moved in together. Our bedroom would fit only a full-size bed and there was no room for nightstands, so I focused on the headboard. A neutral, rectangular headboard was the first non-vintage, non-IKEA furniture purchase we made together, and I paired it with—you guessed it—my black-and-white photos above the bed.

When I was designing our current bedroom, I knew that two things were true: (1) Syd prefers moody elements, and (2) I am revived by natural light. I chose a tall, upholstered headboard in a moss-green Belgian linen to speak to Syd's design preferences, and then I painted our vaulted ceiling a soft greige to keep the space feeling airy for me. Moody floral shams are the bridge between our aesthetics; a thread, quite literally, that ties the entire room together.

Blending styles requires give-and-take but also connection. I have designed hundreds of bedrooms since. All the ingredients have stayed the same—the bed, the rug, the storage, the wall decor—but I have never run out of combinations. Connecting styles through thoughtful decision-making creates more-inspired designs. And inspired designs foster rest, rejuvenation, and an overall sense of well-being.

When designing our floor plan, we were able to push the primary bedroom to the back of the house, giving us room for a vaulted ceiling and an opportunity to utilize an existing chimney flue to add a fireplace. The fireplace is more than heat during the winter; it is a visual cue to settle in and get cozy.

Since the launch of Studio McGee, Syd and I have been knee-deep in building, fixing, and growing our business. Often the only time for peace and quiet is at the end of the day after we've put the kids to bed. The vision for this space was more about creating a feeling than incorporating specific design elements.

TIP: Look for opportunities to tie design features to one another. The textural band on the lamp relates back to the vestibule walls, and the tones of the rug echo the color of the bed.

Sight lines in a home are key to creating a full experience. What could have been a basic hallway is now an extension of our bedroom that makes moving from one space to the next more enjoyable. We have a vestibule leading into our primary bedroom, and I started by designing floor-to-ceiling paneling to dress the space. I kept going back to the drawings because they felt too simplistic. The idea came to me to mimic a reeded furniture detail in the space, so our contractor cut hundreds of half-round trim pieces to achieve the effect. I grow tired of many things very easily, but this wall treatment is not one of them.

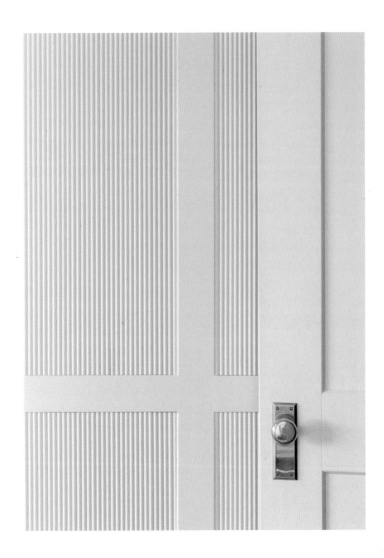

Equal parts modern and feminine with a nod to the coast, this primary bedroom hits all of the notes our clients were after. When working with contrasting styles in a bedroom, we start with a transitional bed that can transform depending on the pieces we pair it with. Here, we customized a canopy bed stocked in solid fabric for a one-of-a-kind look that acts as a unifier for the color palette in the room. Black window frames and a stained ceiling provided a decidedly more modern aesthetic to build upon, so we added softness through more traditional lighting fixtures and decor choices like the leaned-figure sketch and tied velvet bolster pillow. One of the challenges when designing this space was the placement of the door into the bedroom. In order to center the bed under the vault, we were left with a small space for a nightstand on the left and a generous space to the right. We opted to forgo symmetry in favor of a more intentionally filled space. A narrow nightstand on the left hosts a tall, brass task lamp to balance a bedside desk and graceful chair.

TIP: When working with mismatched bedside tables, keep lighting heights as even as possible.

Only one glance at this bedroom and you can feel the Southern California sunshine pouring in through the steel French doors. Our client wanted a room with "a bit of beach and a bit of romance." Bleached jute and a traditional antique rug with a swirling border set the foundation for the pairing of styles on display in this room.

Glass lamps help clear the visual space on the narrow nightstand, and the curved-back velvet sofa on tapered legs fills the length of the room without feeling bulky.

TIP: If you have already mixed two styles of shaded lamps in a room, try incorporating a metal task lamp.

I like to think of designing a home in terms of rhythm rather than cohesion—

it's about movement, cadence, *and* flow.

I like to think of designing a home in terms of rhythm rather than cohesion—it's about movement, cadence, and flow. In a home with light walls in the main open spaces, we decided to change the rhythm and add depth in this primary bedroom. The addition of grass-cloth wallpaper feels like a warm blanket on the walls and is a welcome change of pace. Luxurious layers of down, linen, and wool on the bed complete the look.

When working with bedside sconces instead of table lamps, styling becomes a
key tool to fill the gap above the nightstand. Leaned artwork or a tall vase are
a couple of our go-to picks.

TIP: Articulating sconces keep the nightstand surface clear and add sculptural interest.

With its easy drape and perfectly imperfect rumpled quality, the nature of linen is both laid-back and elegant. Design is as much about what you choose to add to a room as it is what you decide to leave out. This space is not about glitz and glamour. In fact, the goal was the opposite: eliminate all shine and use matte finishes and textures to maintain a calm and relaxed atmosphere.

We used the essence of linen to inspire this primary bedroom through adding layers upon layers of this classic material in different applications. From the drapes and headboard to the bedding, pillows, cloth-covered nightstands, and settee at the foot of the bed, each piece works together to envelop the senses in a dream state.

TIP: Mid-century chairs are one of my favorite foolproof ways to add a modern surprise to any space.

In our basement bedroom, I opted to embrace the lower light and wrap
the room in a swath of hazy wallpaper. To extend the ceiling height visually,
the drapery is on a track system suspended from the ceiling.

Hundreds of pounds of Douglas fir beams connected with steel strappings are the main feature in this room, and it was our job as the designers to have the furniture complement but not compete with the architecture.

TIP: Creating a reading or lounge nook is the best use of an unused bedroom corner. Start with a cozy chair and layer in a floor lamp, a side table, and artwork.

Bathrooms

CHAPTER 07

Bathrooms

Thoughtful design helps elevate even the most routine, everyday experiences.

They may be utilitarian, but you will still find me waxing poetic about bathrooms. In fact, it is because of their mundane necessity that they deserve just as much attention as the other spaces in the home. Thoughtful design helps elevate even the most routine, everyday experiences. Whether the bathroom is seen by guests, shared, or your own spa-like sanctuary, it can make or break one's perception of the home.

Throughout my career I have designed hundreds of bathrooms, from primary suites to powder rooms. In one of my very first custom-home builds, I nearly choked when I realized that there were ten bathrooms to design in one home. My first thought was *How am I going to design more bathrooms in one home than I have in my entire career?* The answer: the same way we approach any bathroom design—by beginning with the end.

Start with visualizing your needs for the space—from your morning skin care routine to hanging your robe to managing how to share it with a significant other—and then bring beauty to the function through each carefully considered selection.

The main components of a bathroom—plumbing, mirrors, lighting, tile, counters, and hardware—stay consistent across a wide spectrum of budgets, styles, and square footage. This

perspective should give novice designers confidence and experienced designers a nudge to push themselves with the selections and details. Materiality is the difference between a sad bathroom and a splendid one.

When I was designing our home, I put a significant amount of thought into where to play it safe and where to take risks. I didn't want my home to be devoid of personality, but I also didn't want to rip out all the tile in a few years because trends change, or my own opinion does. I decided to choose classic shapes for big-ticket items like plumbing fixtures and countertops but push the envelope in smaller spaces like the powder room and kids' bathroom.

Classic selections keep a bathroom grounded, but diving into the minutiae keeps a design from feeling safe (in other words, boring). I give you permission to fuss over the details! Design is the one area of my life where overanalyzing has served me well. Be attentive to opportunities to make tweaks, and be deliberate in your decision-making. This is, after all, the space where you will live your life. If done correctly, the result will stand the test of time while still feeling unique to you.

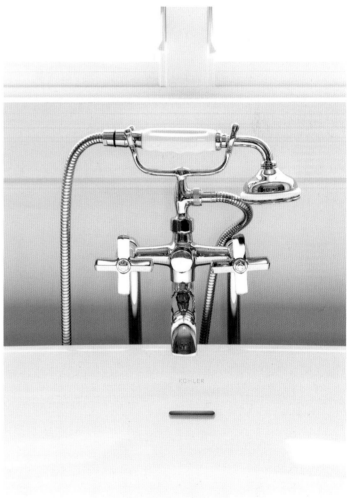

TIP: Stacking two similar artwork pieces is a great way to fill a blank wall space. In our primary bathroom, these sketched seascapes bring a peaceful feel to the room.

Our client was looking for understated glamour with grounding natural elements. The raised paneling, reeded drawer fronts, and classical fixture shapes dress up the foundation of the room while the smooth limestone floors and patina of the freestanding tub provide an organic counterbalance.

TIP: If there is a small space left in the footprint of your bathroom, consider a freestanding piece of furniture rather than more cabinetry. Furniture lends more opportunity for added character.

Simple Shaker cabinets are brought to life with green paint and custom apron-front marble sinks. In this primary bathroom, matching rather than mixing the metals created an opportunity for impact with the warmth of the brass.

TIP: Think outside of the box with hardware placement. We placed pulls across the bottom row to spice up classic form.

In our daughter Wren's bathroom, I designed a vanity using a fluted detail I saw on a vintage dresser. I think furniture is one of the best places for inspiration when designing bathroom cabinetry because small details can be taken and applied in many forms. After selecting classic hexagon tile on the floor, marble on the counters, and a white terra-cotta brick tile for the walls, I knew there was something missing and that the space needed more personality. I made an eleventh-hour decision to carry a rose-hued border around the entire room and was sweating the decision until I saw the result. The reward was worth the risk. The French floral painting I found on Etsy a few weeks later was further confirmation!

If you take a look at the bigger picture, it is imperfections—from the off-center roof pitch we discovered during demolition to the tumbled stone floors with their craggy edges and shade variation—that make a design resonate. So often, we search for clear-cut wood species devoid of knots and movement, but in this bathroom it was quite the opposite: we wanted the minimalist cabinetry to showcase the marks, scuffs, and dings. After pushing for the imperfect, we swung the pendulum in the opposite direction to create balance through crisp contrast and clean lines.

TIP: There is often an awkward space left next to a freestanding tub. Creating a niche with floating shelves provides additional storage and an aesthetic display.

If there is one room in a home where the sentiment "go big or go home" applies, it's the powder room. The smallest space with the most visitors, a powder room is well-served by good design that ensures a pleasant experience. In our powder room, a leafy grass-cloth mural offers verticality to the limited square footage. A floating stone sink suspended from the wall creates a modern statement from a traditional material.

Rift-sawn oak cabinetry is adorned with flush-mount hardware for an elevated take on industrial design. Limestone tiles in random lengths contrast against the clean lines throughout.

TIP: While hanging curtains in the bathroom may not seem necessary, they add warmth and frame the bathtub visually.

Ivy's bathroom can be seen from the entrance to her bedroom, and I wanted the vanity elevation to pop rather than fade against the white walls of her room. I had filed away this swatch of Pimpernel wallpaper years ago waiting for the perfect client, but late one night while stuck on her bathroom design, I realized the answer had been close all along. After hours of forcing the design to fall into place, I scrapped the board and pulled the selections together within minutes.

TIP: Look to history for answers. Shapes, styles, and tones with historical references to time periods you admire will provide confidence in the fact that your design will have longevity.

The first time I toured this mid-century bathroom, there was a sunken in-ground tub, a toilet inside of a clothes closet, and a mishmash of finishes. We gutted everything and reconfigured the layout to include modern-day luxuries like dual sinks, a bidet, and a freestanding tub separate from the shower. We installed terrazzo tile on the floors and a deep green tile across the entire back wall to create a bold statement that connected with the trees beyond the angular window. The brass flower sconce and rust velvet vanity stool are unpredictable pieces that incorporate our clients' love for quirky touches.

Overlooking a backdrop of Swan Lake in Minnesota, this bathroom was designed to feel as though one were getting ready in the woods but with all the luxuries of home. The greenery seen through the floor-to-ceiling picture windows is just as much a part of the design as the freestanding tub.

TIP: Keep the bathroom finishes streamlined when the view is the focal point of the room.

A cleverly designed vanity provides closed and open storage while still offering the sleek impact of floating cabinetry. The finishes in this space were designed to melt together for a spa-like experience. The glass pendant over the tub fills the space without overpowering the room.

TIP: Unexpected furniture pieces in a bathroom can round out the space, add functionality, and provide a place for styling pretty essentials.

BATHROOMS

Workspaces

CHAPTER 08

Workspaces

I want my clients, and myself, to feel inspired, efficient, and accomplished.

When Syd and I first started working together, we took over a guest bedroom and placed two desks opposite each other so that the two of us were staring straight into the walls as we worked. I had a pinboard above mine filled with fabric swatches, magazine tear outs, and inspiration images. There were ubiquitous piles of samples, papers, and loose clips on my side; but on his, he had a large-scale framed constellation print and a single pen. The space was so tight that we had to take turns standing up so the backs of our chairs wouldn't bump into each other. The difference between our desks speaks volumes about how our brains function. Yet somehow, we made it work.

Making it work, or making *you* work, is the core objective of designing an office. But I want it to be so much more than that. I want my clients, and myself, to feel inspired, efficient, and accomplished.

Custom built-ins are the cornerstone of most of our office designs at Studio McGee. They provide storage, opportunities to display items, and additional working surfaces. Functionality informs the layout and foundational pieces, but passions and interests should inform everything that follows. The craving for inspiration opens the door for injecting more personality through large-scale artwork; stronger, bolder colors; and permission to incorporate stuff for the sake of stuff.

Although most workspaces we design are stand-alone rooms, there are many opportunities to carve out desk space where there previously was none. Really, all it takes to create an office area in a nontraditional way is a sliver of empty wall. The thought process when designing a workspace next to a bed, behind a sofa, or in a small nook is the opposite of designing a designated room because the goal is to add a workspace seamlessly, to meld instead of standing out. It is the way we decorate around it that can make or break the experience of the room as a whole.

As we've built Studio McGee, Syd and I have worked from both nontraditional and traditional offices in and out of the home, shared and not. We now have our own offices at home and in the studio, and the experience walking into each is reflective of our individual styles, business roles, and needs to get things accomplished in the ways that inspire us most. I have learned from each design and through years of working within them that it doesn't take much more than a clear surface to make great things happen, but what we choose to surround ourselves with has a profound impact on the experience of getting there.

Syd's office is right off our entryway behind custom oak doors with reeded panels, a subtle detail carried into multiple rooms of our home. After sharing an office with me for so many years, he wanted a man cave—dark, moody, and filled with reminders of his favorite people, places, and sports.

TIP: Dive in to what makes a person tick, their hobbies and passions, to use as inspiration for office decor.

Most of the spaces I design start with a plan that then gets implemented in full, but my studio was (very) slowly assembled with pieces and inspiration I've been collecting over time—and it still has space to bring in what I might pick up tomorrow. That's exactly how I want the studio to feel: like a rotating gallery of what I'm loving at the moment.

Nestled above the garage, the room has a unique architecture and floor plan that adds character but also some complexity. I really wanted to lean in to the studio's "old attic" essence, so we followed the contour of the roof lines, built collar ties across the vaulted ceiling, and added shiplap throughout. In this case, the white wide-plank shiplap lent a historical feel appropriate for the architecture of the space. This light and airy backdrop is a perfect blank canvas for when I bring in samples and lay everything out on my worktable.

A vintage rug informing the color palette and a seating area in the nook next to the door have become a sweet spot for my girls to come chat with me and do their homework.

Know how you focus. I love to lay out my samples on a large surface, but I need to face a window or wall to concentrate, so I added a small desktop in the corner of the room.

TIP: In small spaces, a pair of ottomans is more versatile than a coffee table because they can be moved around easily for surface area, footrests, or seating.

Graphic black-and-white lines are offset by golden white oak furniture and herringbone floors in this modern office space. When chasing this aesthetic, curation is key. With no place, layer, or accoutrement to hide, each item's form must be able to stand alone and in harmony with the other selections. In this space, lighting is the main feature and the punch of red on the desk legs offers just the right amount of surprise.

TIP: Integrate light fixtures into built-ins for ambience and additional visual contrast.

In my office at our headquarters, floral wallpaper and a reeded glass built-in offer the familiar feeling of home in a corporate setting. The slanted shelves with folded brass sconces are a clever way to display books as art.

Our aim when styling this office space was to create a subdued atmosphere inspired by a rainy day curled up at home. We maintained a tight color palette inspired by the finishes and designed the furniture and decor to melt into the backdrop rather than pop.

A small space at the top of the stairs, which was initially intended for a long stretch of linen storage, became the perfect opportunity to incorporate a desk for our clients' young children. Last-minute pivots often become our favorite surprises in a home.

Last-minute pivots often become our favorite surprises in a home.

TIP: Painting the back of a built-in is a great place to experiment with a bold color without covering the entire room.

With French doors on three sides of this office space, we floated the furnishings in the center of the room with lounge seating for guests or to use when a break is needed from desk work. The decor scheme was inspired by the antique easel found during a sourcing trip to Round Top, Texas, to use as a clever display for rotating an ongoing collection of art.

Utility Spaces

CHAPTER 09

Utility Spaces

*Thoughtful designs blend solutions
that bring functionality with visuals
that bring joy.*

Muddy shoes on the floor, scattered backpacks, and yesterday's socks aren't glamorous, but they're life. And as I have said from the beginning, when the humdrum of the everyday isn't feeling pretty, we can always look for ways to make life beautiful. And perhaps it's the challenge of finding beauty in our day-to-day that makes utilitarian spaces like mudrooms and laundry rooms some of my favorites to design.

Whether it's installing a more decorative hook for your coats or designing custom cabinetry with a designated place for everything, there are solutions both simple and extravagant to elevate household duties.

When building our home, I was more excited about having a mudroom than anything else. Lockers! Baskets! A sink! I was looking forward to having a place for everything and being able to hide all the snow gear and shoes. The placement needed to connect to the main house from the garage, ultimately becoming the most-used entrance in our home. We also wanted to be able to access our backyard and use this space as a potting station for our maybe-someday garden. Knowing that it would be a major thoroughfare serving so many purposes, I opted for closed storage to hide clutter and left only a few choice spots open for baskets and display.

The storage decisions were easy for me: just hide everything. It was the combination of countertops and paint colors that took some time. I wanted to be greeted by natural light from all angles, so I created a sight line from our living room to a quaint Dutch door and added windows that extended down to the countertops, choosing sunshine over additional storage.

I had the drawings completed for months, ensuring our storage needs were met, before selecting paint colors. I toyed with pulling in a color from the kitchen because the two rooms were so close, but that felt like a safe decision. Ultimately, I tied the tone of the kitchen into the herringbone floors, a decision that allowed the rooms to connect without being an exact match. The dark-navy cabinetry topped with black soapstone adds drama without sacrificing any of the functionality that we require of the space.

When designing utilitarian spaces, list your priorities so you can be sure to incorporate the top three into the room, and leave room for a few decisions to bring in styling elements that aren't all business. Thoughtful designs blend solutions that bring functionality with visuals that bring joy.

Tumbled limestone pavers, zinc lanterns, and painted-wood knobs lend
an English-country feel to our laundry room. When building our home,
I measured the rolling hampers I intended to use and incorporated them
into the cabinetry design.

TIP: When working with awkward corner situations, I prefer to have the cabinetry extend into the corner with shelving. Here I did a mix of open and closed storage that extends to the countertop.

A remodel of a narrow laundry room was an opportunity to lean in to the quirks and layer on the charm. Rather than following the rule that all cabinets must go to the ceiling, we lowered them to make sense of the ceiling slope, and I couldn't have planned a better result.

During the cabinet phase, it's easy to become consumed in the designs, but I always like to pause and make sure we think ahead to the furniture to make sure we incorporate other materials and textures. Here, the built-in lockers provide all the storage needs, but the freestanding leather bench adds comfort to the space.

Patterned cement tiles offer interest without being overly trendy in this laundry room. Soapstone countertops tie in to the black windows, and a mix of streamlined and throwback details like louvered doors work together in harmony.

TIP: A rustic console table makes an excellent folding table when the cabinet budget is tight or you're looking to infuse character.

A black tongue-and-groove ceiling is dramatic without saturating the entire room. An indoor-outdoor rug is practical for cleanability but also adds warmth and subtle pattern to a contemporary space.

This locker room is the hub of activity for a large family that needed closed storage to hide the chaos of backpacks, coats, and sports equipment. Stone-paver floors provide a historical foundation to the design and a practical way to hide dirt tracked in and out of the home. We included vent cutouts and brass mesh to not only add interest to the white cabinetry but also for the sports gear to air out.

Simple forms become more powerful when we play with proportion. A thick concrete countertop is the centerpiece of this laundry room, with rustic cabinets and modern tile as the ideal complements. We integrated the sink out of the countertop material to be completely seamless for a more modern look.

Simple forms become more powerful when we play with proportion.

TIP: Changing the layout of basic tile is a great way to create interest without increasing the cost. Here we stacked the tile instead of doing a traditional brick-lay application.

In this home, we designed a combined laundry and mudroom adjacent to the garage. This maximized the footprint and versatility for spaces with overlapping functions.

Kids' Spaces

CHAPTER 10

Kids' Spaces

When designing rooms for little ones, my goal is to provide a sense of whimsy and room to grow.

Those with children will know that the old adage is true: growing up happens in the blink of an eye. One moment you're soothing them to sleep in the nursery, and the next you're moving out their crib and finding a spot to display their rock collection. Syd and I are experiencing firsthand with our three daughters—Wren, Ivy, and Margot—how quickly it happens.

When designing rooms for little ones, my goal is to provide a sense of whimsy and room to grow. For example, when the fascination with fire trucks and fairies fades, it's easy to swap out the artwork and accessories or even repaint the walls, but the bed and dresser are investments that grow with the child.

With our oldest two daughters, I've learned to employ the same method for designing their rooms as I do to getting ready with them in the morning. That is, I provide only good options. If their closet has a plethora of curated options, they're more likely to feel empowered in making outfit choices we can all agree upon without a power struggle. In their rooms, I provide choices from selections I know will flow with the design of the rest of our home and have staying power but will also fit with their personalities and ages.

In our home, Wren wanted white, gold, pink, and blue, so we picked pillow options, the chandelier, and accessories together to ensure she was involved in the process. Ivy's only request was a princess bed. Instead of something she's sure to grow out of, I brought in a four-poster washed-oak canopy bed and layered it with patterned sheets, frilly shams, and whimsical accent pillows.

This approach has served our team at Studio McGee well, as some of our clients' custom homes take years to build and design, and the rooms we created in the beginning can be updated easily without a full revamp.

I try to never use the word *should* when it comes to kids' rooms, because many people have different ideas about what they "should" be. Whether it's loud, soft, colorful, or calming, you know what aesthetics are best for your children and your lifestyle. The principle of selecting foundational pieces with longevity and being trend-forward in the accents can be a guiding force regardless of your parenting and design style, and it's a mindset that can be applied to any room of the home.

Wren's room had a large offset window on the back wall that looked good from the exterior of the home but felt lopsided on the interior plans. I decided to design a built-in with a desk on one side to make the window placement feel intentional.

Ivy's room features a canopy bed, or, as she calls it, a princess bed. I added a blush-pink tufted cushion with ties to fasten to the headboard for added comfort while we're snuggled up reading in her bed.

TIP: Create a vignette above your nightstand by hanging a small piece of artwork instead of a standard picture frame.

The rooflines in Margot's room reminded me of a converted attic space, so rather than attempting to disguise the ceiling, I decided to make it a feature. I added tongue and groove and painted it mauve, which felt both unpredictable and fitting for a vintage-inspired nursery. I took a more-is-more approach to the pattern-play with layers of neutral florals, block prints, and gingham textiles.

TIP: If you have low-pile carpet, layer a rug to add pattern and a grounding feature to the space plan.

We like to think beyond flat artwork in kids' spaces and come up with creative solutions for adding dimension and whimsy. In this space we hung footballs above the bed and shelves for leaned books on the wall.

YOU CAN'T CONTROL THE WIND,
BUT YOU CAN ADJUST YOUR SAILS.

This hangout space incorporates zones for both lounging and homework. Instead of traditional wall decor, we intentionally selected unframed flags and lacrosse sticks for a casual vibe. The shadows that fall through this wall of windows are art itself.

The shadows that fall through this wall of windows are art itself.

This playroom infuses earthy olive greens and sky blues that speak to the surrounding landscape in a youthful way. I love a play table on casters—it can be mobile throughout the home and double as a kids' dining table when needed.

TIP: We never miss the opportunity to incorporate baskets when styling kids' spaces. And with the right balance, toys make excellent styling objects too.

Tonal wood-grain wallpaper and whitewashed timbers help rustic feel refined in this mountain retreat.

We wallpapered the ceiling to feel like the night sky in this bunk room and played with different combinations of white and wood throughout—from the niches to the railing and the stairs.

With a hanging chair in one corner and pale-pink clouds on the ceiling, this preteen's bedroom hits the right notes of youth and sophistication. The artwork above the woven bed is the unifying element between the textiles with tones and textures pulled from its palette.

In this teen boy's room, we found a vintage basketball chart online and took inspiration from its curved formations, carrying the theme to the bed, sconces, and nightstand.

TIP: Lamps are the finishing touch to nearly every desk we style due to their height, scale, and architectural shape.

This bedroom is soft and sweet with pink brushstroke wallpaper, a semicircle rattan headboard, and scalloped chandelier. We used side tables instead of nightstands to keep the room feeling light.

The Art *of* Home

CHAPTER 11

The Art of Home

The art of home is a journey filled with nuance and a vision fulfilled with care.

As a designer I always have my favorite vantage points in the homes we design, a place where you stand and it all comes together. Styling is the last step in my design process, a bridge between the home, its furniture, and the people who live within it.

Styling is more art than science and requires patience and devotion to collecting, editing, and shifting. For months, our styling team at Studio McGee works with our clients to understand their interests and preferences so they can incorporate the clients' collected pieces seamlessly with new ones. Our aim when styling is to create a home that looks put together over time rather than in the week it actually takes to install the furniture and accessories.

There are guidelines to follow, but in the end, it's about listening to your gut. For me, I know in my gut that a vignette is right when I don't think about it anymore. My mind won't rest until it just feels right. One of the best tips I can offer you is to have the strength to step away from what you're working on to clear your mind and distract yourself, and then come back to it.

Once the art is hung and the books are placed, I want to be able to take a photograph of every shelf vignette and the room as a whole and find beauty in all of it. This is when I know the styling is complete. However, the real piece of advice I can give is that styling should never be complete. After spending hours staring at your open shelves, don't be afraid to let your home evolve with you. It is an interactive piece of art that unfolds over time. As you collect a new piece of art from the flea market, pick up a new dish on your travels, or receive a new book from a friend, your home and shelves should shift to include the newcomers.

The styling in my home is a compilation of antiques I've collected over the years, pieces I've designed, sentimental keepsakes, and items I incorporated purely because I liked how they looked. There's no wrong choice here—an item that speaks to you may mean nothing to someone else.

Styling requires no special degree or permits, so let your guard down and try it out. Often, I rotate smaller items seasonally to incorporate new color palettes, textures, and trends, or completely change my mind about a piece I've had forever. This ever-evolving environment keeps me stimulated and inspired. It's the place to end your design project and also the best place to get started.

TIP: When a coffee table has a shelf, anchor the look by placing the largest items on the bottom and styling with groupings on top.

TIP: Consider styling the top of a cabinet to draw the eye up and create a more eclectic look.

THE ART OF HOME

TIP: Modern side chairs are a
welcome addition to any style
of dining room.

TIP: A pair of chairs at the foot of the bed is a great alternative to the more ubiquitous bench.

TIP: When designing outdoor spaces, I prefer working with coordinating sets for the main pieces and adding dimension through the accents.

The art of home is a journey filled with nuance and a vision fulfilled with care. Care for the details and care for the people who live there.

There is a point somewhere along the design process when you cross the threshold of a house and it becomes a home. It is beyond the measuring and drawings and the mood boards. It is long after the framing, when the walls begin to take shape and the light is still peeking through the rafters.

Things start to come together when you can hear the scraping of the drywall knife and peel the paper off the floors—but still, not yet a home. When the moving trucks pull into the driveway, you turn the lock, and the home smells of fresh paint, you are on the edge of creating something beautiful—but still, not yet a home.

Home is somewhere between the first smudge on the wall and the crooked family picture that never seems to quite straighten out. A house becomes a home when you know who is running up the stairs just by the sound of their feet. A house becomes a home when the frame on the shelf is filled with a moment you never want to forget.

Home is a place you spend time with the people you love and are surrounded by the things that inspire you. The magic happens at the intersection of beauty and livability. The art of home happens when you make it.

Style Guide
A visual resource for design and decorating

Upholstery Fabrics
Synthetic and Semisynthetic

TIP: Performance fabric is a label used to describe materials that traditionally use one or more synthetic fibers to create a durable, stain-resistant fabric.

FABRIC	PROS	CONS
Polyester	A durable fabric that's resistant to stains, fading, and wrinkling. Great for high-traffic pieces. Offered in a variety of blends with natural materials to improve performance.	Can have an inexpensive look and feel if you're not selective.
Nylon	Often mixed with other fibers to share its durable qualities. It is cost-effective, resistant to snags and wrinkles, and is easy to clean.	Not soft to the touch.
Rayon	Derived from wood pulp, this fabric is then treated to be a less expensive, more durable alternative to silk. It drapes well and has a soft look and feel. Best for drapery and lighter-use applications.	In addition to staining easily, it's not water-proof and loses its original appearance quickly. Works in small doses, but I prefer to use it when blended with other materials.
Microfiber	A polyester blended with polyamide for an ultralightweight fabric that is resistant to everything from water and stains to wrinkles and pilling.	Can have an inexpensive look and feel if you're not selective.
Olefin	Recyclable, colorfast, durable, and resistant to water, fading, and stains. Good for upholstery that will endure a lot of use.	Limited variety of styles. Oil stains can be tough to remove.
Acrylic	A strong fabric that is a great option for both indoor and outdoor applications. It dries fast, is easy to clean, and is resistant to fading.	Prone to pilling and is not resistant to abrasion.
Vinyl	Cost-effective, durable, and cleanable.	Can feel sticky. Has a less sophisticated look and feel than leather. Best used in small doses if the project warrants it.
Crypton	A blend of materials with patented technology that is resistant to water, stains, mildew, and fading. Easy to clean.	More expensive than other options on the market and uses chemicals.

Upholstery Fabrics
Natural

FABRIC	PROS	CONS
Linen	Known for its timelessness and unpretentious beauty, this fabric is my personal favorite. It is strong, drapes well, and is resistant to pilling.	Is not stain resistant and wrinkles easily (which I find to be a positive for more relaxed styles).
Wool	Soft and warm with insulating properties. Textural; durable; resistant to mildew, fading, and wrinkles.	Can be expensive.
Cotton	One of the most common fabrics in the market suitable for almost all interior applications. It is offered in a wide variety of colors, weights, and patterns.	Stains and wrinkles easily.
Silk	Lush and luxurious.	Expensive and susceptible to fading, wear, and snagging.
Leather	A classic, durable upholstery material that can last for many years. It is allergen resistant and relatively easy to maintain.	In addition to being expensive, it is susceptible to scratches, splitting, and cracking.

Pairing Seating Styles

When establishing seating pairings for both living and dining rooms, create connection through contrast. I look for points of cohesion and tension between pieces. The goal is to create enough tension to keep the room interesting while establishing enough of a relationship for cohesion in a space. I like to pull all my options onto a digital whiteboard so I can play with different pairings until I strike a balance that fits the overall mood of the room. There are four design elements I like to contrast when coupling furniture: material, form, scale, and tone.

Create connection through contrast.

Material

Juxtaposing textures helps your home feel more collected and intentional. I like to think in terms of touch and feel—rough versus smooth is a great jumping-off point. For example, a linen sofa pairs well with a velvet love seat; an oak dining chair sits nicely next to a woven one. And a bouclé lounge chair can live in the same room as a leather ottoman. Not every pairing needs to be extreme as long as it is carefully considered. For example, in a beach home, light fabrics are more suitable than heavy ones, and pairing light woods and woven materials creates balance between selections.

Form

Assess the overall shape of a piece as well as the leg style. Find connections through the shapes and contrast through leg styles. Legs play a huge role in mixing and matching furniture—choosing one piece that extends to the floor and another with stylized legs is a no-fail way to pair furniture. Paying attention to form is also a great checkpoint to refer to your mood board to ensure the styles you're pairing relate back to the intended aesthetic of the space.

Scale

While the scale of your furniture should relate to the overall size of the room, it should also speak to the scale of the other pieces. Dining-chair pairings are traditionally weighted on the ends with smaller side chairs between. However, it almost feels unfair to place tiny side chairs next to generously proportioned end chairs, so I consider it a balancing act to choose pieces that are acquaintances, not strangers. The same concept applies to a living room setting—one piece should not overpower a room but rather sit comfortably with the others.

Tone

While contrasting light and dark is the most obvious way to offer contrast in a space, color is also a great way to bring connection between seating styles. For example, the wood base of a sofa could have a similar tone to the frame of a lounge chair, which brings the eclectic mix of styles together in the space. Another example is using patterned upholstery as a jumping-off point to select complementary seating. Focusing on tones when pairing seating styles is applicable to both fabric as well as wood tones. When pairing wood tones, I aim to get them either very close for a tonal look or the opposite for high-contrast impact. When the wood tones fall in the middle of soft tonality and bold distinction, pairings can often appear muddy or unintentional.

Pattern Mixing

TIP: Consider a throw when deciding the pillow scheme. The drape has a relaxed and comforting effect while adding texture, color, and/or pattern.

01   Identify a color scheme

Identifying a color scheme for your throw pillow combination will make the rest of the process much easier. We like to start by considering which accent colors we want to emphasize or add into the space. Throw pillows are a great way to introduce colors and pattern into a neutral space, create a new palette for changing seasons, or draw visual attention to complementing pieces throughout the room, like artwork or rugs. If you don't have a specific palette in mind, get ideas from your favorite patterned pillow as inspiration for the scheme.

02   Choose an organic print

Organic pillow prints are often multicolored, so we like to choose them first to use as a jumping-off point. Organic prints have movement and are inspired by nature.

03   Add clean lines

Characterized by lines, grids, and repetition—geometrics, stripes, checks, and plaids balance out the movement of an organic print and create tension. Tying in one color from your organic print is a simple rule of thumb.

04   Contrast the scale

Once you have your first few pillow patterns and prints, it's time to play with scale! Look at the scale of your current pillows and choose something contrasting. Whether the pattern is significantly larger in scale or significantly smaller, choosing something with stark contrast will make the look feel more curated and interesting.

05   Incorporate solids and textures

Solid pillows help balance out a pillow combination and allow the patterns to speak for themselves. We use solids in pillow combinations to incorporate texture and ground the overall look. Whether it's a subtle fringe detail or a nubby weave, textural solids will add warmth and complete any pillow combination. Although solid and textural pillows can be used in many ways, we often place them at the back of a combination as the largest pillow in the grouping.

06   Mix in vintage

While vintage textiles fit into the categories above, they deserve a category of their own. The character they bring to a pillow combination—or room, for that matter—is unmatched. Every room we design incorporates at least one. You can shop for the raw textiles online or at flea markets, but there are many shops that take the work out of searching and manufacturing, offering premade vintage pillows.

Pillow Styling

As a general rule of thumb, start with the largest-sized pillows in the back of a sofa or bed, and build a triangle with smaller pillows from there. Typically, two- to four-inch size increments work best for layering pillow combinations.

Sofas

I typically use 4 or 5 pillows on a sofa—symmetry creates a traditional look and asymmetry is more casual.

Sectionals

I use anywhere from 7 to 10 pillows on a sectional—2 on each end and 3 in the corner.

Beds (Twin)

Keep it simple with 1 or 2 decorative pillows in addition to the sleeping pillow and sham.

Beds (Queen / King)

I use 3 to 5 decorative pillows in addition to the sleeping pillows and shams. If you're going for a minimalist aesthetic, use one long lumbar across the bed.

Rug Content

Synthetic

A durable and affordable option that is both stain and shed resistant. Synthetic rugs are man-made and designed to mimic higher-end materials like wool. They are easy to clean and can be used in damp environments, making them the go-to for busy areas, kids' rooms, and outdoor spaces.

Wool

Used for everything from premium hand-knotted rugs to practical machine-made options, wool is the most popular rug material. It is soft and resilient with water- and stain-repellant properties. It can be prone to shedding, especially in the first few months of use. I use wool rugs in every room of the home.

Jute, Seagrass, Sisal

Natural fibers offer earthy tones and textures that pair with a wide range of styles. These natural grasses are strong, making them a great choice for high-traffic areas. Although they are tough, they have a tendency to shed and can be difficult to clean. I like to use these rugs in entryways, kitchens, and layered under vintage rugs.

Cotton

Cotton rugs are a cost-effective option with a laid-back feel. They are often offered in flatwoven styles and used as scatter rugs in entries and kitchens. Cotton rugs don't always wear well, so they're best used in casual spaces.

Hair on Hide

Soft, durable, and textural, hides are generally easy to clean and durable if they are away from damp environments.

PET (Polyethylene)

A type of synthetic material often made from recycled bottles, PET is typically used in outdoor rugs. These rugs are durable, easy to clean, and a great choice for both outdoor and indoor applications.

Viscose

A natural material that is man-made from fibers like wood pulp and bamboo—the result is a silklike texture and feel without the high cost. Viscose tends to wear easily and shed like wool, so it is best for bedrooms and low-traffic living spaces.

Rug Construction

Hand-Knotted

A time-honored craft, this is the most intricate and desired of all rugs. Threads are stretched across vertical looms, and each individual knot is hand-tied by artisans to make a pattern. The number of knots per square inch determines the value of the rug. They are traditionally made from wool and are very long-lasting.

Tufted

Instead of weaving and knots, these rugs are made by punching individual threads through a fabric, and then a backing is applied to secure them into place. They are less time-intensive to construct, so they are typically less expensive than hand-knotted rugs. The rug is then sheared to have a smooth surface. These rugs have a higher pile and a cushioned feel.

Machine-Made

The most affordable type of rug construction, these rugs are power-loomed on large machines in a mesh backing. Typically made from synthetic materials and a good choice for high-traffic areas.

Shag

Made with plush, twisted yarns, these rugs are offered in both machine-made and handmade styles. The high pile on this rug makes it very comfortable and stylized, but they are prone to matting over time.

Flatweave

These rugs do not have a pile and are often referred to as *kilims* or *dhurries*. They are woven by hand or on a machine without a backing, making them reversible. This aesthetic tends to be more casual in nature.

Hand-Hooked

These rugs are constructed similarly to a tufted rug but are left unsheared at the end, giving them their looped appearance. The result resembles textural embroidery.

Rug Sizing

Sofas & Sectionals

Placement

Either all legs, or the front two legs should be on the rug.

Spacing

Your rug should extend at least 6 inches beyond the sofa, but 12 inches is ideal. Allow 8 to 24 inches between the rug and edge of the room on all sides. Keep in mind, the coffee table should be about 18 inches away from the sofa.

Orientation

Follow the length of the longest sofa or length of the sectional.

Sizing
Sofas

8 x 10

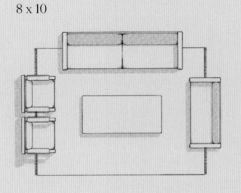

9 x 12

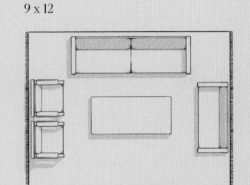

Sectionals

9 x 12

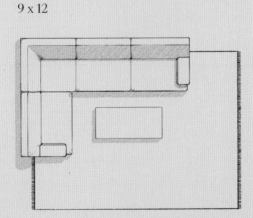

10 x 14

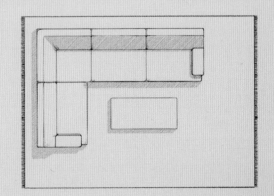

Beds

Placement

Under the lower two-thirds of the bed with a few feet exposed at the foot—this allows room for a bench and to see the rug more clearly. If possible, avoid placing the rug under the dresser.

Spacing

Rug should line up near the edge of nightstands or beyond. Leave approximately 6 to 36 inches between the rug and front of nightstand, depending on the space at the foot of the bed.

Orientation

Perpendicular to the length of the bed.

Sizing
Twin

5 x 8   6 x 9

Full / Queen

6 x 9   8 x 10   9 x 12

King

8 x 10   9 x 12   10 x 14

Dining Tables

Placement

Centered under the table with all legs on the rug.

Spacing

Rug should extend past the table about 3 feet, so there is enough room to pull a chair out to sit.

Orientation

For rectangular arrangements, follow the length of the table. For round, anything goes—the rug orientation depends on the shape of the room.

Sizing
Rectangular

8 x 10

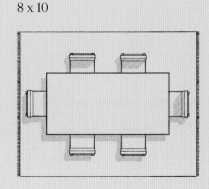

9 x 12

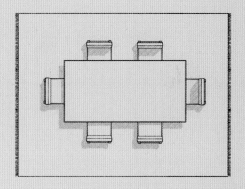

Round

8 x 10

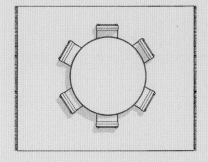

Mixing Metals

Tip: These are guidelines to give you confidence in making selections, but don't overthink it!

| 01 | Narrow your palette | Look for the warm or cool undertones of each finish and how they will pair together. Black works well with any metal. |

01 Narrow your palette

Look for the warm or cool undertones of each finish and how they will pair together. Black works well with any metal.

02 Pick a dominant finish

Pick a dominant finish, an accent, and a bonus.

UNLACQUERED BRASS

AGED BRASS

POLISHED NICKEL

CHROME

SATIN NICKEL

BLACK

OIL RUBBED BRONZE

03 Consider the placement

Group metals according to their application. The most popular approach in kitchens is matching the hardware and lighting using the dominant finish and incorporating a different metal on the faucet and appliances.

04 Create balance

Spread the dominant finish throughout to create impact rather than clustering a metal in one corner of a room. A great way to tie the room together is to include one piece in the space that incorporates two of the metals you are pairing.

Countertops

Edge Profiles

FLAT / STRAIGHT

EASED

BEVEL

QUARTER ROUND

DOUBLE QUARTER ROUND

FULL BULLNOSE

HALF BULLNOSE

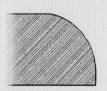

COVE

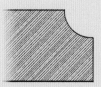

OGEE

DOUBLE OGEE

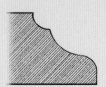

DUPONT

DUPONT + 1/2 BULLNOSE

FRENCH COVE

MITERED

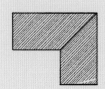

Countertop Materials

MATERIALS	PROS	CONS
Marble	• Natural stone • Timeless • Heat resistant • Wide range of colors and styles • Can be polished or honed • Often considered the most designer look of all options	• Porous surface, meaning it can stain and etch • Scratches and chips • Wide range of price points depending on the type • Requires sealing and maintenance
Quartz	• Engineered material • Stain, scratch, impact, and heat resistant • Variety of colors and styles • Nonporous • No maintenance required	• Designed to mimic natural stone, but it never will be! • Natural stone has a cold temperature to the touch, but quartz has a more manufactured feel • Not a one-of-a-kind selection, which can feel impersonal
Granite	• Natural stone • The most heat resistant natural stone • Nonporous after it is sealed • Wide range of colors and options • Cost-effective	• Speckled appearance versus veining • Porous if not properly sealed
Quartzite	• Natural stone • Heat resistant • Variety of colors and styles • When sealed it is more durable than marble	• Requires maintenance to be sealed • Can be costly depending on the slab
Soapstone	• Natural stone • Timeless • Heat resistant • Does not need to be sealed • Easy to disguise surface scratches with readily accessible products • Typically cost-effective	• Susceptible to scratches and nicks • Narrow range of colors, from gray to black

MATERIALS	PROS	CONS
Butcher Block	• Adds warmth and character • Great for baking • Timeless • Cost-effective	• Requires regular maintence • Scratches and dents easily
Concrete	• Modern aesthetic • Stain, heat, and water resistant when sealed • Customizable thickness, profiles, colors, and textures	• Ages over time • Prone to stains, scratches, chips • Requires maintenance
Limestone	• Natural stone • Timeless • Typically cost-effective	• Limited colors ranging from creams to grays • Requires maintenance • Stains and etches
Porcelain	• Engineered stone made from clay-based materials • Veining and colors are very realistic • Nonporous, scratch and stain resistant • Slabs are offered in large sizes • Cost-effective	• Edge styles are limited • Thin material, so seaming on edges can be more obvious

Kitchen Styling

When styling a kitchen, I always remove every item from the countertops and open shelves to provide a clean slate and new perspective. When selecting items to display and others to hide, the deciding factor is always whether the piece blends both form and function. Depending on the scale of the kitchen, we use some, or all, of these tips in every kitchen we design. The groupings work time and time again, but the actual selection of the items is what lends personal style and relates back to the design of the home.

Group	Create a grouping of essentials near the stove. A few ideas here are a crock, spoon rest, and oil and vinegar bottles.
Gather	Corral loose items with a tray.
Lean	Lean breadboards to fill an empty backsplash.
Fill	Utilize jars or canisters for dry goods, like flour or oatmeal, and to hide candy.
Level	Add a tall vase for height and a bowl nestled next to it on an island or peninsula. Choose decor that looks good filled or alone.
Display	Display a few of your favorite cookbooks in the corner, propped open on a stand, or stacked under a beautiful bowl.
Use	If you have open shelves, keep the most-used items on the bottom shelves and the lesser-used kitchen pieces above.
Simplify	Keep the sink simple with items that are both functional and aesthetically pleasing.
Layer	Layer in a kitchen towel and runner by the sink or stove for color and pattern.
Elevate	Think outside of the box and add in an item or two purely for elevating the look—a small piece of artwork or sentimental vase.
Add	Add life with potted herbs and fresh flowers.

Coffee Table Styling

TIP: Walk around all sides of the table when you're finished to ensure it looks great from all angles.

01 Set the foundation with trays and books

Creating a base to build off of is important when designing anything, but especially when styling a coffee table. I like to work with an odd number of groupings. One of the easiest ways to start is with a tray. Not only do trays bring the perfect focal point or base, but they are great for corralling everything that ends up there, whether that's a candle, coasters, or a stray remote.

02 Add levels

Whether your coffee table is big or small, it's always a good idea to have some varying levels to bring interest. Playing with height doesn't have to mean only fresh greenery—taper candles, an empty vase, and stacked boxes work too.

03 Layer in objects

Placed alone or on top of books, decorative objects are the best way to add some interest to your coffee table.

04 Vary the shapes

Pay attention to mixing round and rectangular shapes for balance.

Bed Styling

01 Create a base with sheeting

First things first: creating a base of comfort for your bedding is essential. Crisp, soft, or textural linen, sheets should be based on client preference rather than style—a classic sheet pairs well with anything layered on top.

02 Layer with a luxurious duvet

Duvet covers do not need to match the sheets; rather, they need to coordinate. Folding duvets once or twice provides the fluffy appearance that entices you to dive right into bed.

03 Fold in coverlets or quilts

Next, we add a coverlet or quilt to create a warm, comfortable setting. There are many ways to style a bed, but I usually place a quilt under the duvet or a coverlet on top. You can use one or both depending on the location of the home and how much additional warmth is needed. In homes with consistently warm temperatures, I will forgo this layer altogether. I also make these decisions based on what color or pattern I want most prominent in the design scheme.

04 Add pillows and shams

I like to use two sleeping pillows and two shams that fit the length of the bed. I stack or prop them against the headboard depending on the look I'm chasing. Typically, I match the sleeping pillows to the sheets and the shams to the duvet, but there is no hard rule here, and it's fun to mix it up.

05 Bring dimension with decorative pillows

Now it's time for the fun part! Whether it's a stacked-pyramid look or a simple long lumbar, adding throw pillows brings more dimension by introducing texture, pattern, and color. (Read more about pillow styling on page 367.)

06 Complete the look with a soft throw

Lastly, adding a throw to the end of a bed adds an extra hint of texture and functionality for cooler nights or midday naps. The draped effect also lends a more lived-in aesthetic.

Shelf Styling

TIP: It helps to place similar objects at the same time. For example, style all of your baskets, then your vases, and so on.

01 Start with a blank canvas

No matter what kind of shelves we're styling, we begin by removing everything and starting with a blank canvas. That way, we can see the space we're working with in a new light.

02 Take inventory

Evaluate what you're working with to set yourself up for success. With all your decor spread out on the floor, you can get a good look at your options and organize them by size. Need some inspiration for what to display? Try a mix of these:

- Books
- Bookends
- Vases
- Framed photos
- Artwork
- Baskets

- Boxes (individual and stacked)
- Candles
- Potted plants
- Dishes and bowls
- Accent objects

03 Lay the foundation with substantial pieces

Placing your biggest pieces first will ground the look and create focal points. We recommend staggering them in order to balance the visual weight across the shelves. Vases, baskets, bowls, leaned artwork, or other large decor items are perfect for adding substance and visual weight to a built-in.

04 Create groupings with your smaller items

This next step can be the hardest part of the process but also the most rewarding! I love to create groupings of 2 or 3 items to fill in the spaces that large pieces don't occupy. A few easy ways to do this are stacking books (horizontally or vertically), pairing a taller and shorter vase together, and layering decor on top of books. This is also the perfect time to add personal touches like family photos or collected objects to make it your own!

05 Step back to gauge balance and levels

After you create vignettes and find a new home for all of your odds and ends, now it's time to step back and see the bigger picture. Varying the shapes, heights, and even the textures will bring an overall sense of balance and interest to the room.

06 Edit, adjust, and circle back

Styling feels best when you shift pieces around, leave them alone for a bit, and come back to revisit. If you feel stuck, step away and come back with fresh eyes—this is a trick for novices and experienced professionals alike.

Lighting Heights

Dining

For standard 8-foot ceilings, plan for 32 to 36 inches between the top of the table and bottom of the chandelier. Add approximately 3 inches for each foot above 8-foot ceilings.

Lighting Style
Linear Light

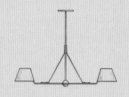

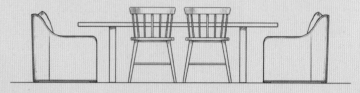

Pendant Light

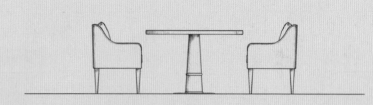

Chandelier

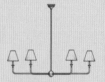

Ceilings over 10 feet

Add together the width and length of the room in feet for the approximate diameter needed in inches. The bottom of the light should be approximately one-third of the ceiling to the floor. For a more specific measurement, start with 7 feet and add 3 inches for every foot over 8-foot ceiling height.

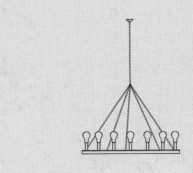

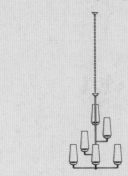

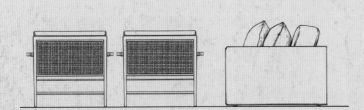

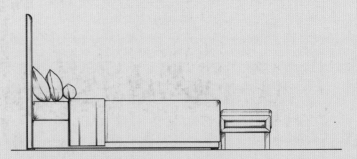

Ceilings under 10 feet

Hang your light fixture with a 7-foot to 7.5-foot clearance below.

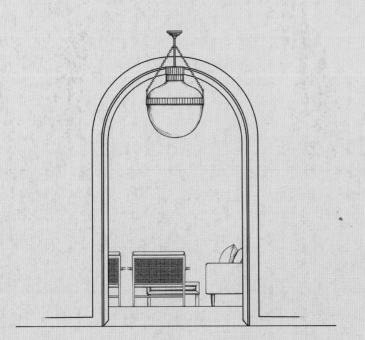

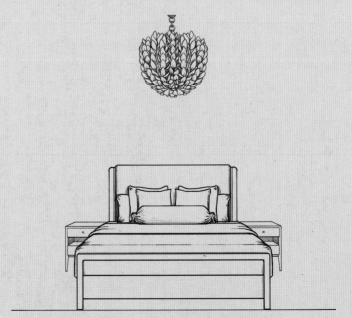

Kitchen Islands

For standard 8-foot ceilings, hang kitchen pendants 30 to 36 inches above the island. Add 2 to 3 inches for every foot above 8 feet. The widest part of the pendants should be approximately 30 inches apart. Allow for at least 6 inches on each end of the island.

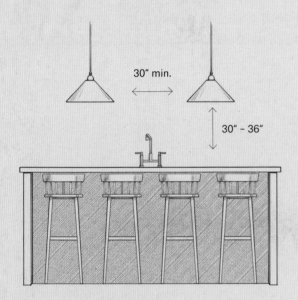

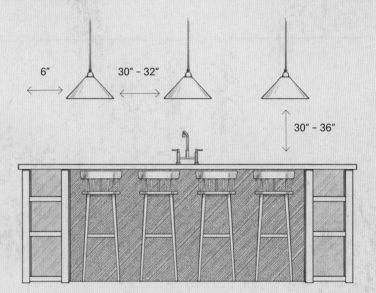

Hanging Artwork

On a blank wall

60 inches from floor to center of artwork

Above a console or sofa

Approximately two-thirds of the width of furniture below

In groupings

2 to 3 inches between art

Paint

White

Chantilly Lace	Benjamin Moore
Simply White	Benjamin Moore
Timeless	Clare Paint
White Dove	Benjamin Moore
Cloud White	Benjamin Moore
Swiss Coffee	Benjamin Moore
Alabaster	Sherwin-Williams
Greek Villa	Sherwin-Williams
Ivory Lace	Sherwin-Williams
Shaded White	Farrow & Ball

Gray

Classic Gray — Benjamin Moore

Natural Cream — Benjamin Moore

Edgecomb Gray — Benjamin Moore

Gray Owl — Benjamin Moore

Repose Gray — Sherwin-Williams

Revere Pewter — Sherwin-Williams

Chelsea Gray — Benjamin Moore

Kendall Charcoal — Benjamin Moore

Down Pipe — Farrow & Ball

Cheating Heart — Benjamin Moore

Beige

String   Farrow & Ball

Wool Skein   Sherwin-Williams

Grant Beige   Sherwin-Williams

Manchester Tan   Benjamin Moore

Natural Linen   Sherwin-Williams

Kilim Beige   Sherwin-Williams

Shaker Beige   Benjamin Moore

Antler Velvet   Sherwin-Williams

Relaxed Khaki   Sherwin-Williams

Accessible Beige   Sherwin-Williams

Green

Pigeon — Farrow & Ball

French Gray — Farrow & Ball

Intrigue — Benjamin Moore

Sea Haze — Benjamin Moore

Dark Olive — Benjamin Moore

Nitty Gritty — Portola Paints

Salamander — Benjamin Moore

Studio Green — Farrow & Ball

Dried Thyme — Sherwin-Williams

Vintage Vogue — Benjamin Moore

Blue

	Skylight	Farrow & Ball
	Light Blue	Farrow & Ball
	Boothbay Gray	Benjamin Moore
	Wolf Gray	Benjamin Moore
	De Nimes	Farrow & Ball
	Hague Blue	Farrow & Ball
	Midnight	Benjamin Moore
	Railings	Farrow & Ball
	Hale Navy	Benjamin Moore
	Deep Royal	Benjamin Moore

Black

Peppercorn   Sherwin-Williams

French Beret   Sherwin-Williams

Off Black   Farrow & Ball

Wrought Iron   Benjamin Moore

Iron Ore   Sherwin-Williams

Tricorn Black   Sherwin-Williams

Black Magic   Sherwin-Williams

Black Beauty   Benjamin Moore

Green Black   Sherwin-Williams

Soot   Benjamin Moore

Acknowledgments
& Credits

It is my design philosophy that a home comes to life in the in-between moments, and that is exactly how this book came to fruition—between making lunches, reading bedtime stories, filming a television show, and running multiple businesses. My heart has been buoyed along the way by my husband, Syd, and our children, Wren, Ivy, and Margot. Thank you for being the constant inspiration for what home means to me.

My words may fill the pages of this book, but there are many creators, collaborators, and clients who have helped turn this vision into a reality.

Thank you

Kortney Eggertz, for sharing your talent and dedication, and for thoughtfully designing each page of this book.

Lucy Call, for your storytelling behind the lens. I am in awe of your perspective and ability to capture the essence of each moment we design, both large and small.

Kristine Metcalf, you evoke the feeling of home through every vignette you create. It has been a joy to experience this journey together since the early days of Studio McGee.

Kelsie Lindley, for your commitment to creating beauty over the years by leading projects and our design team, and for considering the details down to a fraction of an inch.

Studio McGee Team, for your creativity and connection to the homes we design. You pour yourselves into these homes from before they even break ground, and it shows. And to the many team members orchestrating the facilitation of these projects behind the scenes.

Studio McGee clients, for trusting the process, even when the revelation feels a thousand miles away.

Harper Horizon team, for being open-minded to our ideas, collaborating with us, and supporting this endeavor.

Bill Stankey, for thinking big, your unwavering support, and always being willing to make things happen.

Lacy Morris, for your offer to lend your expertise. It changed my outlook in the last sprint to completion. I am grateful for your edits and feedback, which elevated the copy of this book.

Madison Sumsion, for the organizing, scheduling, communicating, and never-ending encouragement.

Mom and Dad, for bolstering my spirit every step of the way and influencing my love for art, style, and, most important, home.

BECKHAM HOME
Location: Utah
Builder: Flagship Homes
Photography: Lucy Call
Interior Finishes: Studio McGee
Design & Styling: Studio McGee
Seen On: 364

COTTONWOOD KITCHEN REMODEL
Location: Utah
Builder: Killowen Construction
Photography: Lucy Call
Interior Finishes: Studio McGee
Design & Styling: Studio McGee
Seen On: 152–55, 378

CRESTVIEW HOME
Location: Southern California
Architect: Eric Olsen Design
Builder: Dagan Design & Construction Inc.
Photography: Ryan Garvin
Interior Finishes: Studio McGee
Design & Styling: Studio McGee
Seen On: 66–67, 69, 132–35, 200–3, 238–39, 298–99

HILLTOP ESTATE
Location: Southern California
Architect: Hart Howerton
Builder: Lombardi Construction
Photography: Lucy Call
Interior Finishes: Studio McGee
Design & Styling: Studio McGee
Seen On: 28, 42–43, 45, 52, 60–61, 63–65, 88–91, 108, 126–31, 156–59, 164–67, 180–81, 196–97, 199, 222, 230–33, 292–93, 316–19, 321, 360, 372, 408

HISTORIC CHARLESTON REMODEL
Location: Utah
Builder: Killowen Construction
Photography: Lucy Call
Interior Finishes: Studio McGee
Design & Styling: Studio McGee
Seen On: 48–51, 100–3

HOMESTEAD PROJECT
Location: Arizona
Architect: Poca Architecture + Design, LLC
Builder: Gather Projects
Photography: Lucy Call
Interior Finishes: Studio McGee
Design & Styling: Studio McGee
Seen On: 82–85, 172–75, 234–35, 322–25

HOME ON THE BAY
Location: Northern California
Architect: Holscher Architecture
Builder: Sausalito Construction
Photography: Lucy Call
Interior Finishes: Studio McGee
Design & Styling: Studio McGee
Seen On: 40–41, 92–95, 118–21, 160, 182–85, 210–13, 242–43, 277, 300–1, 342–43, 390

HOME ON THE RANCH
Location: Utah
Architect: Hebdon Studios
Builder: Everlast Custom Homes
Photography: Lucy Call
Interior Finishes: Studio McGee
Design & Styling: Studio McGee
Seen On: 138–39, 141, 296–97, 336–37

MCGEE HOME
Location: Utah
Architect: Lloyd Architects
Builder: Killowen Construction
Photography: Lucy Call
Interior Finishes: Studio McGee
Design & Styling: Studio McGee
Seen On: 12, 16, 18, 21–22, 25–27, 36, 38–39, 54, 56–59, 110, 113–117, 148–51, 162, 188, 190, 192–95, 214–17, 224, 226–29, 236–37, 240–41, 244–45, 256, 258–65, 282, 284, 286–87, 302, 304, 306–15, 353, 363, 370, 376, 396, 403

MCGEE & CO. SUMMER 2021
Location: Virginia
Architect: Sagatov Design + Build
Builder: Sagatov Design + Build
Photography: Lucy Call
Interior Finishes: Studio McGee
Design & Styling: Studio McGee
Seen On: 348–49, 358

MCGEE & CO. OUTDOOR 2021
Location: Southern California
Architect: Roberto Moreno (remodel, 2008)
Glen C. McAlister (original, 1928)
Photography: Lucy Call
Staging & Styling: Studio McGee
Seen On: 350–51

MCGEE & CO. FALL 2021
Location: Northern California
Architect: Bryant M. Paul (1928)
Builder: KSM Construction
Photography: Lucy Call
Interior Finishes: Brodie Jenkins
Staging & Styling: Studio McGee
Seen On: 382

MCGEE & CO. SUMMER 2022
Location: Northern California
Architect: Warren Charles Perry
Photography: Lucy Call
Staging & Styling: Studio McGee
Seen On: 10, 356, 366

MCGEE & CO. FALL 2022
Location: Utah
Architect: Tiek Design Group
Builder: Mike and Jenna Rosa
Photography: Lucy Call
Interior Finishes: Mike and Jenna Rosa
Staging & Styling: Studio McGee
Seen On: 362

MCGEE & CO. WINTER 2022
Location: Utah
Builder: Grove Homes
Architect: Tiek Design Group
Photography: Lucy Call
Interior Design: Ali Henrie
Staging & Styling: Studio McGee
Seen On: 272–75, 346–47, 363, 368

MCGEE & CO. SPRING 2023
Location: Sonoma, California
Architect: Steve Brown & Leah Anderson Designs
Builder: Steve Brown & Leah Anderson Designs
Photography: Lucy Call
Interior Finishes: Steve Brown & Leah Anderson Designs
Staging & Styling: Studio McGee
Seen On: 2, 4–6, 31, 34, 96–99, 176–79, 278–81, 338, 340, 344–45, 362, 367, 384–86

MID-CENTURY MODERN BATH
Location: Utah
Builder: Killowen Construction
Photography: Lucy Call
Interior Finishes: Studio McGee
Design & Styling: Studio McGee
Seen On: 246–47

MOUNTAINSIDE RETREAT
Location: Utah
Architect: Lloyd Architects
Builder: Jackson Leroy
Photography: Lucy Call
Interior Finishes: Studio McGee
Design & Styling: Studio McGee
Seen On: 46–47, 104–7, 144–47, 206–9, 294–95

PARK CITY CONTEMPORARY HOME
Location: Utah
Architect: Otto-Walker Architects
Builder: Craig Construction
Photography: Lucy Call
Interior Finishes: Studio McGee
Design & Styling: Studio McGee
Seen On: 74–77, 122–25, 186–87, 252–53, 328–29, 388, 394

RANCH HOME
Location: Utah
Architect: Line 8 Design
Builder: Russell & Co. Construction
Photography: Lucy Call
Interior Finishes: Studio McGee
Design & Styling: Studio McGee
Seen On: 70–73, 142–43, 170–71, 218–21, 290–91, 326–27

RYE HOME
Location: New York
Architect: RMG Associates
Builder: Edgewood Contracting Corp.
Photography: Lucy Call
Interior Finishes: Studio McGee
Design & Styling: Studio McGee
Seen On: 78–81, 266–67, 332–35

STUDIO MCGEE HEADQUARTERS
Location: Utah
Builder: Killowen Construction
Photography: Lucy Call
Interior Finishes: Studio McGee
Design & Styling: Studio McGee
Seen On: 254, 268–71

SUNSET HOME
Location: Utah
Architect: Flagship Homes
Builder: Flagship Homes
Photography: Lucy Call
Interior Finishes: Studio McGee
Design & Styling: Studio McGee
Seen On: 330–31

SWAN LAKE HOME
Location: Minnesota
Architect: PKA Architecture
Builder: Elevation Homes/Streeter Custom Builder
Photography: Lucy Call
Interior Finishes: Studio McGee
Design & Styling: Studio McGee
Seen On: 248–51

WINDSONG HOME
Location: Utah
Architect: Tiek Design Group
Builder: Tiek Built Homes
Photography: Kate Osborne
Interior Finishes: Studio McGee
Design & Styling: Studio McGee
Seen On: 288–89

INTERIOR SKETCHES
Illustrations: Mat Edwards
Seen On: 373–75, 391–93, 395

Shea McGee is a *New York Times* bestselling author and the creative visionary behind Studio McGee Inc.

Shea McGee is a *New York Times* bestselling author and the creative visionary behind Studio McGee Inc., a multidisciplinary design business encompassing interiors, products, and entertainment. She founded the business out of a spare bedroom with her husband, Syd McGee, in 2014 and has since grown into one of the most prolific names in the industry. As a designer, entrepreneur, and mother of three girls, Shea has inspired millions to make life beautiful. She has led the design of hundreds of homes across the country and is known for creating timeless custom interiors that feel effortless. Their loyal fanbase and ever-expanding design portfolio paved the way for the launch of their e-commerce brand McGee & Co. as well as partnerships with Target, Kohler, and Ann Sacks. In 2020, Shea and Syd premiered their reality show, *Dream Home Makeover*, on Netflix, showcasing Shea's signature style in everything from one-bedroom renos to multimillion-dollar estates. With a vision that beautiful design can be approachable, Studio McGee has become one of the most highly sought-after interior design destinations for clients and fans who love their light-filled aesthetic.